# MacBook Air®

## PORTABLE GENIUS
## 3rd EDITION

by Paul McFedries

WILEY

John Wiley & Sons, Inc.

MacBook Air® Portable Genius, 3rd Edition

Published by
John Wiley & Sons, Inc.
10475 Crosspoint Blvd.
Indianapolis, IN 46256
www.wiley.com

Published simultaneously in Canada

ISBN: 978-1-118-18618-3

Manufactured in the United States of America

10   9   8   7   6   5   4   3   2

For general information on our other products and services or to obtain technical support, please contact our Customer Care Department within the U.S. at (877) 762-2974, outside the U.S. at (317) 572-3993 or fax (317) 572-4002.

John Wiley & Sons, Inc. also publishes its books in a variety of electronic formats and by print-on-demand. Not all content that is available in standard print versions of this book may appear or be packaged in all book formats. If you have purchased a version of this book that did not include media that are referenced by or accompany standard print version, you may request this media by visiting http://booksupport.wiley.com. For more information about Wiley products, visit us www.wiley.com.

Library of Congress Control Number: 2011940393

WILEY

# About the Author

**Paul McFedries** is a technical writer who has been authoring computer books since 1991 and has more than 70 books to his credit. Paul's books have sold more than four million copies worldwide. These books include the Wiley titles *Teach Yourself VISUALLY Mac OS X Lion, Switching to a Mac Second Edition, iPad 2 Portable Genius, iPhone 4 Portable Genius,* and *The Facebook Guide for People Over 50.* Paul is also the proprietor of Word Spy (www.wordspy.com), a website that tracks new words and phrases as they enter the language. You can visit Paul on the web at www.mcfedries.com or on Twitter at www.twitter.com/paulmcf and www.twitter.com/wordspy.

# Credits

**Senior Acquisitions Editor**
Stephanie McComb

**Project Editor**
Chris Wolfgang

**Technical Editor**
Paul Sihvonen-Binder

**Senior Copy Editor**
Kim Heusel

**Editorial Director**
Robyn Siesky

**Business Manager**
Amy Knies

**Senior Marketing Manager**
Sandy Smith

**Vice President and Executive Group Publisher**
Richard Swadley

**Vice President and Executive Publisher**
Barry Pruett

**Project Coordinator**
Sheree Montgomery

**Graphics and Production Specialists**
Noah Hart
Andrea Hornberger

**Quality Control Technician**
Melissa Cossell

**Proofreading and Indexing**
Debbye Butler
BIM Indexing & Proofreading Services

For Karen.

# Acknowledgments

When guests to our house would learn that I was writing a book about MacBook Air, their eyes would invariably light up. Ah, I'd think, they're impressed that I'm writing a book! Alas, no: "Ooh," they'd say, "Can I see it?"

They meant, of course, MacBook Air, and so I'd trot it out so everyone could coo over it, and my wife's carefully planned dinner party would devolve into a geekfest for awhile. That was just one of the perks of writing this book.

Another was working with the amazing folks at Wiley, all of whom are preternaturally nice. They include Acquisitions Editor Stephanie McComb and Executive Acquisitions Editor Jody Lefevere, who asked me to write the original version of this book the same day that MacBook Air was announced, and of course I accepted about 5 seconds later; Project Editor Chris Wolfgang, whose edits, suggestions, and questions showed not only her smarts and utter common sense, but also her knowledge of what a book needs to make it better; Copy Editor Kim Heusel, who went beyond merely crossing my t's and dotting my i's by using her keen eye to tighten my prose and make me look good in print; and Technical Editor Paul Sihvonen-Binder, a deep source of knowledge regarding all things Mac, who made generous use of that knowledge and his valuable time to supply this book with a layer of wisdom beyond what its author possesses.

Finally, many thanks to the wonderful Karen Hammond, who took the marvelous photographs that are sprinkled throughout this book. My heartfelt and deep thanks to all of you for your tremendous work on this project.

# Contents

## chapter 11

How Do I Solve Specific Software
Problems?

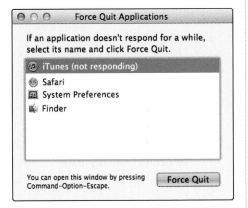

## chapter 12

How Do I Solve Specific
Hardware Problems?

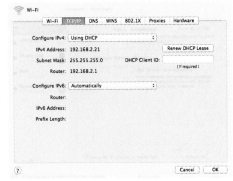

# Introduction

**Back in 2008,** I bought one of the original MacBook Airs, and it quickly became my go-to Mac notebook. It was light as a feather and impossibly thin. The screen was gorgeous, the Multi-Touch trackpad was a lot of fun, and even the keyboard wasn't bad at all. No wonder my trusty MacBook Pro started gathering dust!

So, in mid-2011, when Apple came out with its latest version of the MacBook Air that had a backlit keyboard (yes!), a full-featured Multi-Touch trackpad, faster memory, the option to add more memory (up to 4GB!), a faster processor, longer battery life, Thunderbolt support, and it was both lighter and (gasp!) thinner, well, can you say "no-brainer"?

Fortunately, I haven't been disappointed: The new MacBook Air is a fantastic machine. However, it's not (yet) a perfect machine. Yes, the two USB ports are a huge help, but it's still a challenge to connect FireWire devices given the lack of a FireWire port. You need MacBook Air on your super-fast gigabit network to transfer some stuff, but there's no network port in sight. The Thunderbolt port is great if you have a Thunderbolt monitor, but it's a head-scratcher if you're trying to connect to a DVI or VGA monitor, or to a TV. And Apple hasn't made it any easier to get inside this thing!

Not only that, but MacBook Air runs OS X, of course, so it comes with the limitations and annoyances of that operating system. Yes, it's mighty simple to use out of the box, but some of its most useful and powerful features are hidden away in obscure parts of the operating system. Sure, OS X doesn't get in your way when you're trying to be productive or creative, but sometimes it does something (or forces you to do something) that just makes you want to raise your eyebrows in wonderment. MacBook Air's robust design makes it a reliable machine day after day, but even the best-built machine can have problems.

When you come across a conundrum or problem, either with MacBook Air itself or with OS X, you might consider making an appointment with your local Apple Store's Genius Bar. More often than not, the on-duty genius could give you good advice on how to overcome the conundrum or solve the problem. The Genius Bar is a great thing, but it isn't always a convenient thing. You can't just drop by to get help — you have to make an appointment. You have to drag yourself down to the store, perhaps wait for your genius, get the problem looked at, and then make your way back home. In some cases, you may need to leave MacBook Air for a day or two while the problem gets checked out and, hopefully, resolved.

What MacBook Air users really need is a version of the Genius Bar that's easier to access, more convenient, and doesn't require tons of time or leaving MacBook Air in the hands of a stranger. What MacBook Air users really need is a "portable" genius that enables them to be more productive and solve problems wherever they, and their MacBook Air, happen to be.

Welcome, therefore, to *MacBook Air Portable Genius, 3rd Edition*. This book is like a mini Genius Bar all wrapped up in an easy-to-use, easy-to-access, and eminently portable format. In this book, you learn how to get more out of MacBook Air by learning how to access all of the really powerful and timesaving features that aren't obvious at a casual glance. In this book, you learn how to avoid your MacBook Air's more annoying character traits and, in those cases where such behavior can't be avoided, you learn how to work around it. In this book, you learn how to prevent MacBook Air problems from occurring and, just in case your preventive measures are for naught, you learn how to fix many common problems yourself. And, yes, this book also shows you how to get inside MacBook Air's case!

This book is for MacBook Air users who know the basics, but want to take their education to a higher level. It's a book for people who want to be more productive, more efficient, more creative, and more self-sufficient (at least as far as MacBook Air goes, anyway). It's a book for people who use MacBook Air every day, but would like to incorporate MacBook Air into more of their day-to-day activities. It's a book I had a blast writing, so I think it's a book you'll enjoy reading.

You love MacBook Air because it doesn't require you to be a genius to accomplish basic, everyday tasks. Got a new mouse? Just plug it into one of the USB ports and it's ready to use within seconds. Nice! Unfortunately, some devices are more ornery and require a bit of extra effort on your part to get them connected and configured. In this chapter, I take you through connecting a few such devices, including Thunderbolt devices, an external display, another Mac, a printer, and imaging devices such as digital cameras and scanners.

# Connecting Thunderbolt Devices

Connecting external devices to a computer has always suffered from two problems: speed (or lack thereof) and convenience (or lack thereof). The speed issue is an ancient one, and interface designers have been slowly increasing the pace at which various technologies transfer data. For example, USB has gone from a pokey transfer rate of 12 megabits per second (Mbps) in version 1.0, to 480 Mbps in 2.0, and 5 gigabits per second (Gbps) in 3.0. Similarly, FireWire has gone from 400 Mbps in FireWire 400 to 800 Mbps in FireWire 800.

The convenience issue is more complex:

- **Compatibility.** Although newer interface standards are usually backward-compatible with earlier standards, devices designed for the old standard often require an adapter. For example, adding a FireWire 400 device to a FireWire 800 port requires a FireWire 800-to-400 adapter cable.

- **Connections.** Interface connections can be maddeningly inconsistent. USB is the main villain here, with legions of different device-side connectors, including Micro, Mini, Standard-A, Standard-B, and so on.

- **Driver support.** Device driver support can be shaky, particularly with newer technologies. For example, USB 3.0 devices often lack the drivers required to take full advantage of the interface's new features.

- **Port availability.** This can be problematic, depending on the computer. This is particularly true on the MacBook Air, which includes just two USB ports and no FireWire ports. On many computers, particularly notebooks, if you need to connect multiple external devices, you often need to use a hub.

Compare all this with the current state of the art in *internal* device connections: PCI Express. This interface is widely used (all Macs, including MacBook Air, use PCI Express internally), it's blazingly fast (up to 16 Gbps), and device drivers are easy to come by.

The performance and convenience gap between internal and external connections has never been more of a concern because nowadays we're not just connecting keyboards and mice: We're adding peripherals such as external hard drives, RAID arrays, Ethernet cards, and video capture devices that scream for as much throughput as you can give them. What the world needs is an external device interface that's both super fast and super convenient.

Welcome, then, to the new world of Thunderbolt. Developed by both Intel and Apple, Thunderbolt effectively combines both PCI Express and Apple's Mini DisplayPort display technology (which I discuss in more detail in the next section):

Thunderbolt port

**1.1** The latest version of the MacBook Air comes with a Thunderbolt port for connections to external displays and other devices.

- **Speed.** Thunderbolt offers two data channels, each of which supports 10 Gbps throughput.

- **Flexibility.** Thunderbolt supports not only data transfer components such as hard drives and video capture devices, but also high-resolution displays.

- **Compatibility.** A Thunderbolt port is the same size and shape as a Mini DisplayPort (see Figure 1.1), so devices designed for Mini DisplayPort, such as the Apple LED Cinema Display, can plug right in. Similarly, adapters designed to work with Mini DisplayPort, such as adapters for DVI and VGA displays, will still work with Thunderbolt ports. Unfortunately, devices designed for Thunderbolt will not work with Mini DisplayPort connectors.

- **Connections.** Thunderbolt supports *daisy-chaining*, which means a single port can support multiple devices, up to six at a time. This works because many Thunderbolt-compatible devices come with multiple Thunderbolt ports. For example, take a look at the rear of the Promise Pegasus R4 RAID storage unit, shown in Figure 1.2. As you can see, it includes two Thunderbolt ports. This means you can run a Thunderbolt cable from your Mac to the device, and then run a second cable from the other Thunderbolt port to another device.

Thunderbolt ports

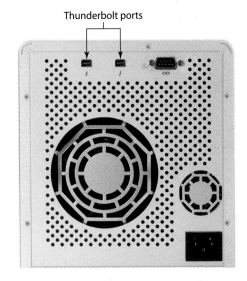

**1.2** Many Thunderbolt devices come with two ports, so you can daisy-chain multiple Thunderbolt devices to your MacBook Air without requiring a hub.

**Note**

The latest 27-inch iMacs also come with two Thunderbolt ports.

The 2011 edition of MacBook Air comes with a single Thunderbolt port (shown earlier in Figure 1.1), so you can use it to connect Thunderbolt devices.

# Connecting an External Display

If you have an extra external display — a monitor, television set, or projector — just lying around, you can connect it to MacBook Air for various scenarios:

- **As an alternative display.** You can use the external display instead of MacBook Air's built-in monitor.

- **As a desktop extension.** You can use the external display to extend the MacBook Air desktop.

Fortunately, both of these connection types are plug-and-play (meaning once you plug in and turn on the external display, MacBook Air recognizes the new device right away). That's the good news. The bad news is that although using an external monitor is plug-and-play, the plug part isn't as straightforward as you might like because there are many ways to connect a MacBook Air to a display. The next few sections provide you with the details you need to make things happen.

## Understanding external display connections

To connect MacBook Air and an external display, you need to know the various ways these connections can occur. The next few sections provide you with the details.

### Thunderbolt connections

As I mentioned earlier, the mid-2011 edition of MacBook Air comes with a Thunderbolt port. Thunderbolt supports both data transfer devices (for example, hard drives and RAID arrays) and high-resolution displays. So if you have a Thunderbolt-compatible display, such as the Apple Thunderbolt Display, you can use a Thunderbolt cable to connect the display to MacBook Air.

If you have a device that uses a different connector type — such as DVI or VGA — you can still use MacBook Air's Thunderbolt port, but you'll need an adapter. Fortunately, existing Mini DisplayPort adapters (which I talk about a bit later) will work just fine with the Thunderbolt port, so you shouldn't have any trouble connecting other displays to MacBook Air.

## Mini DisplayPort connections

On the 2010 edition of the MacBook Air, the display connection was the Mini DisplayPort, which is the same size and shape as the Thunderbolt port shown earlier in Figure 1.1. (The original MacBook Air used a Micro-DVI port.)

You can use the Mini DisplayPort port to connect MacBook Air to external displays that use three connector types: DVI (digital video interface), VGA (video graphics array), and video.

To connect MacBook Air's Mini DisplayPort to an external display, you need at least a Mini DisplayPort cable. If your display supports Mini DisplayPort signals, your work is done. Otherwise, you need to purchase an adapter that converts the Mini DisplayPort signal to video output compatible with your display (as I explain in the next three sections).

1.3 A DVI-A connector.

## DVI connections

The standard video connection type on most LCD monitors and on some televisions and projectors is DVI. That sounds simple enough but, unfortunately, external displays such as LCD monitors and televisions can use different DVI connectors. There are actually three types:

- ⦿ **DVI-A.** This connector works only with analog signals (see Figure 1.3).

- ⦿ **DVI-D.** This connector works only with digital signals. It comes in single-link and dual-link versions (see Figure 1.4).

1.4 DVI-D single-link (left) and dual-link (right) connectors.

**Genius**

What's the difference between single-link and dual-link? DVI uses a transmitter to send information along the cable. A single-link cable uses one transmitter, whereas a dual-link cable uses two transmitters. This means that dual-link connections are faster and offer better signal quality.

⊚ **DVI-I.** This connector works with both analog and digital signals. It comes in single-link and dual-link versions (see Figure 1.5).

As you can see, each type of DVI connector uses a slightly different pin arrangement. When you're matching your external display, DVI cable, and DVI adapter (described next), you need to make sure that they all use the same type of DVI connector.

1.5 DVI-I single-link (left) and dual-link (right) connectors.

**Note**

In high-tech cable and port connections jargon, a connector with pins is described as male and a connector with holes is described as female. Both of the Mini DisplayPort to DVI adapters use a female DVI connector, which means you can't plug either one directly into an external display's DVI port, because it is also female. In other words, you need to run a DVI cable — which is male on both ends — between the adapter and your external display.

To connect MacBook Air's Mini DisplayPort to a DVI port on an external display, you have two choices depending on the type of DVI required by the display:

⊚ **DVI-D single-link.** You need to get the Apple Mini DisplayPort to DVI Adapter.

⊚ **DVI-D dual-link.** You need to get the Apple Mini DisplayPort to Dual-Link DVI Adapter, shown in Figure 1.6.

If the external display uses a DVI-I port, it probably means you have a DVI-I cable, and that cable won't fit either of the adapters' DVI-D connectors. In this case, the adapter on its own won't cut it. To solve the problem, you either need to buy a DVD-D cable, or you need to hunt down a DVI-D to DVI-I adapter so you can use your DVI-I cable.

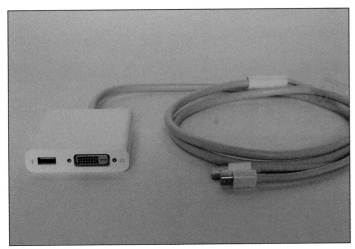

1.6 Use the Apple Mini DisplayPort to Dual-Link DVI Adapter to connect your Mac's Mini DisplayPort to an external display's dual-link DVI port.

**Note**

A dual-link DVI connector plugs into (and works with) a single-link DVI port. Unfortunately, the reverse isn't true; that is, you can't plug a single-link DVI connector into a dual-link DVI port. Note, too, that a DVI-D connector can plug into a DVI-I port, but a DVI-I connector won't fit into a DVI-D port.

## VGA connections

All CRT monitors and many LCD monitors and projectors come with a VGA connector, shown in Figure 1.7.

1.7 VGA connectors are standard on CRT and common on LCD monitors.

9

To connect MacBook Air to an external display that offers only a VGA connector, use the Mini DisplayPort to VGA adapter, shown in Figure 1.8.

## Video connections

If your external display is an older television or projector (or even a VCR), it likely has either a Composite (yellow RCA) connector or an S-Video connector; both are shown in Figure 1.9. To connect MacBook Air to an external display that only offers either Composite or S-Video connectors, use the Mini DisplayPort to VGA adapter, then get a second adapter to convert the VGA signal to the output you require (VGA-to-video adapters are offered by many third-party manufacturers).

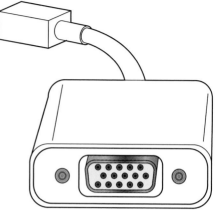

1.8 Use the Mini DisplayPort to VGA adapter to connect the MacBook Air Mini DisplayPort port to an external display's VGA port.

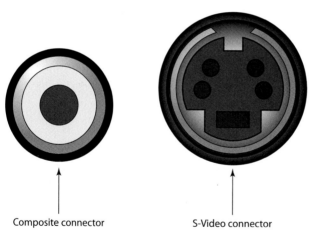

Composite connector          S-Video connector

1.9 Composite (left) and S-Video (right) connectors are common on televisions, projectors, and VCRs.

If your external display is a high-def TV, it most likely comes with an HDMI (High-Definition Multimedia Interface) connector. To connect MacBook Air to an external display that only offers an HDMI connector, you need to get a Mini DisplayPort-to-HDMI adapter. As of this writing, Apple doesn't offer such an adapter, but some third-party companies do, such as the adapter made by Moshi (http://store.moshimonde.com), shown in Figure 1.10 (which is also available through the Apple Store).

## Setting the external display mode

The hard part about using an external display is getting the correct cables and adapters and ensuring they fit into the appropriate connectors, particularly on the display. However, once that is set, the rest is a breeze. As soon as you connect the external display and turn it on, MacBook Air recognizes it and starts using it. That's more like it!

1.10 Use the Mini DisplayPort to HDMI adapter to connect your MacBook Air to an external display's HDMI port.

How you use the external display depends on what you want to do with it. MacBook Air gives you two choices:

- **Video mirroring.** This external display mode means that the same image that appears on the MacBook Air's main or built-in display also appears on the external display. This is useful if you want to use a larger monitor to work with MacBook Air or if you want to show MacBook Air's desktop on a projector so that other people can see it.

- **Extended desktop mode.** This mode means that MacBook Air's desktop is extended onto the external display. This is useful if you need more screen real estate to display your programs. For example, you can have your main application open on one display and an application that you're monitoring — such as Mail, iChat, or Safari — on the other display.

To switch between these external display modes, follow these steps:

1. **Click System Preferences in the Dock.** The System Preferences window appears.

2. **Click the Displays icon.** The display preferences appear, and you see one set of preferences for each screen.

**Genius**

After you connect your external display, you should calibrate the display so that the colors of images appear correctly. To calibrate a display, open its display preferences, click the Color tab, and then click Calibrate. This launches the Apple Display Calibrator Assistant, which takes you step by step through the calibration process.

3. **Click the Arrangement tab to select the external display mode.**

   ● To turn on video mirroring, select the Mirror Displays check box, shown in Figure 1.11.

   ● To turn on extended desktop mode, deselect the Mirror Displays check box.

4. **If you turned on extended desktop mode, use the objects in the Arrangement tab to configure the screen layout (see Figure 1.11).** To set the relative screen positions, click and drag the screen icons to the positions you prefer. To set the location of the menu bar, click and drag the white strip to the screen you prefer.

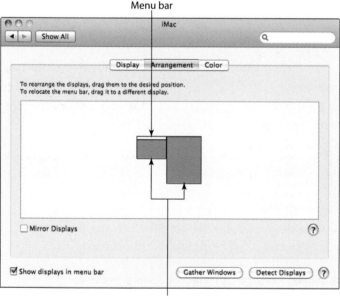

1.11 Use the objects in the Arrangement tab to configure the screen layout in extended desktop mode.

# Connecting MacBook Air to another Mac

If you have another Mac kicking around, it's natural to want to share things between that Mac and your MacBook Air: documents, Safari bookmarks, iTunes libraries, downloads, and more. The standard way of sharing data between computers is to create a network. However, that requires a central connection point for the computers, usually a router.

If you don't have such networking hardware handy (for example, you're in a hotel room or on a plane), you might think that sharing is off the table, but that's not true. There are actually several ways that you can connect two Macs directly: with a Thunderbolt cable, with a network (or crossover) cable, or by creating an ad hoc wireless network. The next two sections provide the Thunderbolt and network cable details; see Chapter 2 to learn about creating an ad hoc wireless network.

## Connecting to another Mac with a Thunderbolt cable

If you have a 2011 MacBook Air and you just happen to have a Thunderbolt cable lying around, that's great because you can use it to connect MacBook Air and another Mac via their Thunderbolt ports and share files between them. I'm assuming here, of course, that the other Mac also comes with a Thunderbolt port (as most recent Macs do).

Besides connecting the two Macs using the Thunderbolt cable, you also have to make sure that your Macs are configured to share files. Follow these steps:

1. **Click System Preferences in the Dock.**
2. **Click the Sharing icon.** The Sharing preferences appear.
3. **Turn on file sharing.**
   - **OS X Lion, Leopard, or Snow Leopard.** Select the File Sharing check box.
   - **Earlier version of OS X.** Select the Personal File Sharing check box.
4. **If you feel like it, you can also use the Computer Name text box to edit the name of your Mac, which is the name that will appear in the Network window of the other Mac.**

To see the other Mac, open Finder and then choose Go⇨Network (or press Shift+⌘+K). Double-click the Mac's icon, click Connect As (in Lion or Leopard) or Connect (in earlier versions), and then type a name and password to connect to the other computer.

## Connecting to another Mac using a network cable

The other way to connect MacBook Air to another Mac directly is to string a network cable between them. A network cable is also called a *twisted-pair* cable (because it consists of four pairs of twisted copper wires that together form a circuit that can transmit data), and it comes with an RJ-45 jack on each end.

Your MacBook Air doesn't come with an Ethernet port, of course, so you'll need to connect an Ethernet adapter to one of MacBook Air's USB ports. A good example is Apple's USB Ethernet adapter, shown in Figure 1.12. One of the network cable's RJ-45 jacks plugs into the Ethernet adapter, and the other connects to the corresponding Ethernet port on the other Mac.

The connection is basically the same as with a Thunderbolt cable, so I'll just give you the barebones steps here (see the preceding section to flesh out the details):

1.12 You can connect MacBook Air to another Mac via a network cable using Apple's USB Ethernet adapter.

1. **Connect the network cable to both Macs.**

2. **Turn on file sharing on both Macs.**

3. **Use Finder's Network window (choose Go⇨Network) to connect to the other Mac.**

# Connecting and Sharing a Printer

Nine times out of ten — it's probably more like 99 times out of 100 — connecting a printer to MacBook Air is a no-brainer: You plug it in to the USB port, turn it on, and presto! MacBook Air and your printer have already become fast friends and you can start printing right away. How can you be sure? You can tell in a couple of ways:

**In any application that supports printing, choose File ⇨ Print.** In the dialog that appears, you should see your printer's name in the Printer list.

**Note** You can also display the list of connected printers from any application that supports printing. Choose File ⇨ Printer, open the Printer list, and then select Add Printer.

● **Click System Preferences in the Dock, and then click Print & Scan.** In the Print & Scan preferences that appear, you should see your printer's name in the Printers list, as shown in Figure 1.13.

**1.13** If MacBook Air recognized your printer, it appears in the Printers list in the Print & Scan preferences.

**Genius** Surprisingly, Windows doesn't have a monopoly on annoying behavior. One of the senseless things that OS X does is set the default printer to whatever printer you used or added most recently. To fix this, choose System Preferences ⇨ Print & Scan. Then, in the Default Printer list, choose the printer you want to use as the default.

## Connecting a printer manually

What happens on those rare occasions when MacBook Air doesn't recognize your printer? In that case, you need to do a bit more legwork and install the printer manually. Here's how it's done:

1. **Connect and turn on the printer if you haven't done so already.**

2. **Click System Preferences in the Dock, click Print & Scan, and then click the + icon.**
   MacBook Air displays the list of connected printers.

3. **Choose your printer.**

   - In Mac OS X Lion, if your printer appears in the list of nearby printers, click it and then skip the rest of these steps; otherwise, click Add Other Printer or Scanner.

   - If your printer shows up in the list of available printers, simply choose it from the list.

   - If you don't see your printer in the list, install the printer driver by hand as follows:

     1. **Insert the disc that came with your printer.** Note that you'll need to connect an external optical drive to your MacBook Air, or use a remote optical drive as described in Chapter 2.

     2. **Choose Other in the Print Using list.**

     3. **Open the printer disc (or the folder where you downloaded the printer driver), choose the printer driver, and then click Open.**

4. **In the Print Using list, choose Select a driver to use and then choose your printer if it is in the list that appears.**

5. **Click Add**. Your printer is now connected.

**Note**

If you don't have an external optical drive or a printer disc, or if the disc doesn't contain MacBook Air drivers, visit the printer manufacturer's website and download the drivers you need. If you can't get drivers for the printer (annoyingly, some printer manufacturers don't bother writing Mac drivers), you may still be able to use the printer by choosing Generic PostScript Printer in the Print Using list.

# Adding a shared network printer

If MacBook Air is part of a network, you have a big advantage. You can connect a printer to one computer, and the other computers on the network can then use that computer for printing. That saves you big bucks because you don't have to supply each computer with its own printer.

To use a shared network printer, you must first add it to MacBook Air's list of printers. Follow these steps if the printer is shared on another Mac (see the next section for Windows printers):

1. **Click System Preferences in the Dock, and then click Print & Scan.**

2. **Click the + icon.**

3. **In Mac OS X Lion, if the network printer appears in the list of nearby printers, click it and then skip the rest of these steps; otherwise, click Add Other Printer or Scanner.**

4. **In the Printer Browser's list of printers, select the shared printer you want to use.** There are two ways to recognize a shared printer.

   - **OS X Leopard or later.** The Kind column displays Bonjour Shared, as shown in Figure 1.14.

   - **Earlier versions of OS X.** The Connection column displays Shared Printer.

5. **Click Add.** You can now use the shared network printer.

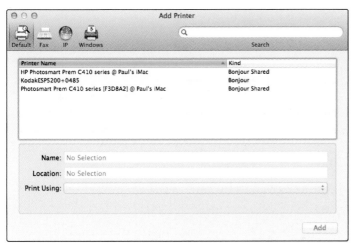

1.14 In OS X Leopard or later, look for Bonjour Shared in the Kind column.

# Adding a shared Windows network printer

If the shared printer you want to use is part of a Windows network, follow these steps to add it to MacBook Air's list of printers:

1. **Click System Preferences in the Dock, and then click Print & Scan.**

2. **Click the + icon.**

3. **In Mac OS X Lion, click Add Other Printer or Scanner.**

4. **Display the list of Windows workgroups on your network.**

   - **OS X Leopard or later.** Click the Windows tab.

   - **Earlier versions of OS X.** Click More Printers and then use the top list to select Windows Printing.

17

5. **Choose the workgroup that contains the computer with which you want to work.**

6. **Click the computer with the shared printer you want to add.**

7. **Log on to the Windows computer.**

8. **Click the shared printer you want to use.** See the example in Figure 1.15.

9. **In the Print Using list, choose Select a driver to use, and then choose the printer in the list that appears.**

10. **Click Add.** You can now use the shared Windows printer.

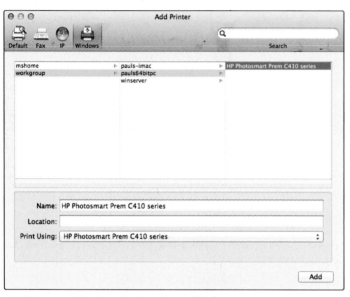

1.15 You can add a shared printer from a Windows computer.

## Sharing your printer with the network

If you have a printer connected to MacBook Air and you'd generously like other folks on your network to be able to use it, you can share it by following these steps:

1. **Click System Preferences in the Dock.**

2. **Click the Sharing icon.** The Sharing preferences appear.

3. **In Mac OS X Lion, click the Lock icon, type your Mac OS X administrative account password, and then click Modify Preferences.** If you're using an earlier version of Mac OS X, you can skip this step.

4. **Select the Printer Sharing check box.**

5. **In the list of printers, select the check box beside the printer you want to share.**

# Connecting and Sharing Imaging Devices

MacBook Air is a graphics powerhouse. You can take advantage of that power by connecting various imaging devices, such as digital cameras, digital camcorders, and document scanners. Most of these devices connect without a hassle. However, you need to watch out for a few things and follow a few extra steps to make sure each device works as it should. In the next few sections, I take you through all of this.

**Genius**

Many digital camcorders require a FireWire connection, but MacBook Air doesn't come with a FireWire port. One solution is to purchase a FireWire-to-USB adapter cable. It connects to the camcorder's digital video FireWire port on one end and to MacBook Air's USB port on the other. Another solution is to purchase a hub that combines both USB and FireWire ports.

## Connecting an imaging device

Connecting an imaging device to MacBook Air is mostly a straightforward bit of business that begins with attaching the device:

- **Digital camera.** Attach a USB cable to the camera and to the USB port on MacBook Air.

- **Digital camcorder.** Attach a FireWire cable to the video camera and to a FireWire port on your Mac.

- **Scanner.** Attach a USB cable to the scanner and to the USB port on MacBook Air. You must also install the software that came with the scanner. This installs not only the device driver, but also the application — sometimes called the TWAIN software — that operates the scanner.

**Caution**

Most FireWire-compatible digital camcorders are compatible with MacBook Air, but not all. For example, most Sony digital camcorders don't work with MacBook Air. If you're looking to buy a camcorder, be sure to do some research on the web to make sure the camera you want is MacBook Air friendly.

19

For most digital cameras and camcorders, MacBook Air immediately connects to the device and perhaps even offers to download images (via iPhoto) or video (via iMovie).

# Connecting to a networked imaging device

When you set up a network, you might expect to share devices such as printers and DVD drives, but did you know that you can also share imaging devices? This is a great feature because it enables you to view and download a camera's pictures, import a camcorder's video, or operate a scanner, all without having any of these devices connected directly to MacBook Air, but to another Mac on your network.

Follow these steps to connect to a shared imaging device in Mac OS X Lion or Snow Leopard:

1. **In Finder, choose Applications ⇨ Image Capture.** The Image Capture program appears.

2. **Click the Shared branch.** Image Capture displays a list of shared imaging devices.

3. **Click the device with which you want to work.** Image Capture displays the device controls, as shown in Figure 1.16.

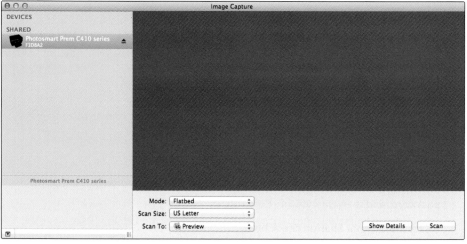

1.16 In Lion or Snow Leopard, click Image Capture's Shared branch and then click the shared imaging device.

Follow these steps to connect to a shared imaging device in OS X Leopard and earlier versions of OS X:

1. **In Finder, choose Applications ⇨ Image Capture.** The Image Capture program appears.

2. **Choose Devices ⇨ Browse Devices (or press ⌘+B).** Image Capture displays a list of available devices.

3. **Double-click the Remote Image Capture devices branch.**

4. **Double-click the branch that contains the imaging device you need.**

5. **Choose the device you want to work with.**

6. **Connect the device.**

   - **OS X Leopard.** Select the check box in the device's Connected column.

   - **Earlier versions of OS X.** Click the Connect button.

# Sharing an imaging device

If you have a digital camera, digital camcorder, or scanner connected to MacBook Air, you can share that device with your network pals.

How you go about this is quite a bit different in Mac OS X Lion and Snow Leopard than in Mac OS X Leopard, which in turn was different than in earlier versions of Mac OS X, so I treat them separately.

First, here's how to share a scanner in Lion and Snow Leopard:

1. **Click System Preferences in the Dock.**

2. **Click the Sharing icon.** The Sharing preferences appear.

3. **In Mac OS X Lion, click the Lock icon, type your Mac OS X administrative account password, and then click Modify Preferences.**

4. **Select the Scanner Sharing check box.**

5. **In the list of scanners, select the check box beside the scanner you want to share, as shown in Figure 1.17.**

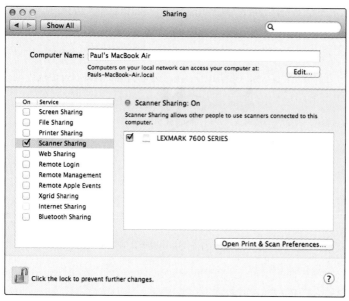

**1.17** Turn on Scanner Sharing and then select the scanner you want to share.

Unfortunately, Mac OS X Lion doesn't offer a way to share a digital camera. Here's how you share a digital camera in Snow Leopard:

1. **In Finder, choose Applications ⇨ Image Capture.** The Image Capture program appears.

2. **In the Devices branch, click your camera.**

3. **Select the Share camera check box.**

Here are the Leopard steps for sharing any imaging device:

1. **In Finder, choose Applications ⇨ Image Capture.** The Image Capture program appears.

2. **Choose Devices ⇨ Browse Devices (or press ⌘+B).** Image Capture displays a list of available devices.

3. **Click Sharing.**

4. **Select the Share my devices check box.**

5. **For each device you want to share, select the check box in the device's Shared column.**

6. **Edit the Shared name if you feel like it.**

7. **If you want folks to type a password to use the devices, select the Password check box and then type your password.**

8. **Click OK.** The Image Capture Device Browser window now appears with a Shared column.

Now here are the steps for sharing an imaging device in earlier versions of OS X:

1. **In Finder, choose Applications ➪ Image Capture.** The Image Capture program appears.

2. **Choose Image Capture ➪ Preferences.** The Image Capture Preferences dialog appears.

3. **Click the Sharing tab.**

4. **Select the Share my devices check box.**

5. **Select the check box for each device you want to share.**

6. **Edit the Shared name if so desired.**

7. **If you want to protect your devices with a password, select the Password check box and then type your password.**

8. **Click OK.**

# How Do I Make Wireless Connections?

That mass of wires and cables under your desk doesn't have a name, although some of the more clever suggestions I've heard are *corducopia*, *quagwire*, and *nerdnest*. In the end, though, it doesn't much matter because, let's face it, wires are *so* last century. Wireless is the way to go, and MacBook Air is designed to thrive in a wireless world. In this chapter, you learn how to take advantage of MacBook Air's wireless features to connect to a network and Bluetooth devices, operate a remote DVD drive, transfer files, and connect to or transfer settings from another Mac.

# Connecting to a Wireless Network

MacBook Air wears its wireless heart on its sleeve by not having an Ethernet port, which all other Macs available today use to make a wired connection to a network switch or router. Instead, MacBook Air comes with a built-in wireless networking card that enables MacBook Air to connect to Wi-Fi (Wireless Fidelity) networks. That's not to say that MacBook Air is incapable of making wired network connections. If you happen to be using a network that doesn't offer Wi-Fi, all you need to do is attach an Ethernet adapter to one of MacBook Air's USB ports. A good example is Apple's USB Ethernet adapter (see Chapter 1).

## Connecting to a Wi-Fi network

However, wireless networking is MacBook Air's forte, so here are the steps to follow to connect MacBook Air to a wireless network:

1. **In the menu bar, click the Wi-Fi status icon.** MacBook Air displays a list of available wireless networks, as shown in Figure 2.1.

2. **Choose the network you want to join.** If the network is password-protected, MacBook Air prompts you for the password.

3. **Type the password.** If the password is long or complex, you can be sure that

2.1 Click the menu bar's Wi-Fi status icon to see a list of wireless networks that are within range of MacBook Air.

you're typing it correctly by selecting the Show password check box. If you're in a public area, it's a good idea to make sure no one can see the exposed password.

**Note**

In the Wi-Fi list, wireless networks that display the lock icon are secure networks protected by a password. To connect to such a network, you need to know the password.

4. **If you want MacBook Air to automatically connect to this network the next time it comes within range, select the Remember this network check box.**

5. **Click OK.** MacBook Air connects to the wireless network.

## Connecting to a hidden Wi-Fi network

Each Wi-Fi network has a network name — often called the Service Set Identifier, or SSID — that identifies the network to Wi-Fi-friendly devices such as your MacBook Air. By default, most Wi-Fi networks broadcast the network name so you can see the network and connect to it. However, some Wi-Fi networks disable network name broadcasting as a security precaution. The idea here is that if an unauthorized user can't see the network, he or she can't attempt to connect to it. (However, some devices can pick up the network name when authorized computers connect to the network, so this is not a foolproof security measure.)

You can still connect to a hidden Wi-Fi network by typing the connection settings. You need to know the network name, the network's security type and encryption type, and the network's password. Here are the steps to follow:

1. **Click the Wi-Fi status icon in the menu bar and then click Join Other Network.** The Find and Join a Wi-Fi Network dialog appears.

2. **Use the Network Name text box to type the network's SSID.**

3. **Use the Security pop-up to choose the type of security used by the Wi-Fi network: WEP, WPA Personal, WPA2 Personal, WEP Enterprise, WPA Enterprise, WPA2 Enterprise, or None.** If you're not sure, try WPA2 Personal, which is probably the most common type for most home networks. If you choose anything other than None, MacBook Air prompts you to type the password.

4. **Use the Password text box to type the password.**

5. **If you want MacBook Air to automatically connect to this network the next time it comes within range, select the Remember this network check box.**

6. **Click Join.** MacBook Air connects to the network.

## Setting up an ad hoc wireless network

If you have another Mac kicking around, it's natural to want to share things, such as documents, Safari bookmarks, iTunes libraries, and downloads, between it and your MacBook Air. The standard way of sharing data between computers is to create a network, in particular a wireless network, for MacBook Air. However, that requires having a central connection point for the network, which in the wireless world means a wireless access point.

If you don't have such networking hardware handy (for example, you're in a hotel room or on a plane), you might think that sharing is off the table, but that's not true. You can create a special wireless network that directly connects the two Macs.

I'm not talking about a standard wireless network that uses an access point (also called an infrastructure wireless network). I'm talking about a *computer-to-computer wireless network* (also called an *ad hoc wireless network*) that doesn't use an access point. As long as you have two (or more) Macs with wireless networking capabilities, it's very easy to set this up:

1. **Click the Wi-Fi status icon in the menu bar and then click Create Network.** The Create a Computer-to-Computer Network dialog appears.

2. **Type a name for the new network in the Network Name text box.**

3. **Leave 11 selected in the Channel list.**

4. **If you want people to type a password to join your network (a good idea), use the Security list to choose either 40-bit WEP (to use a 5-character password) or 128-bit WEP (which requires a 13-character password).**

5. **Type the password in the Password and Confirm password text boxes and click Create.** Your Mac sets up the computer-to-computer network.

To connect to your new network from another Mac, click the Wi-Fi status icon in the menu bar and then click the name of your network, which appears in the Devices section of the Wi-Fi menu, as shown in Figure 2.2.

If you set up a password for the network, you're prompted to type the password.

2.2 Your new ad hoc network appears in the list of available wireless networks.

# Setting Up a Remote DVD Drive

MacBook Air's unofficial title as the world's lightest notebook computer is the result of a lot of hard, creative work on the part of Apple and its partners (including Intel, which built a tiny processor just for MacBook Air). However, that claim to lightweight fame is also the result of quite a few compromises, like not having FireWire or Ethernet ports.

Perhaps the most controversial omission is MacBook Air's lack of a DVD drive. This seems like a huge problem at first, but you probably find that, as you use MacBook Air from day to day, the absence of an optical drive becomes less noticeable. You can always transfer files over a wireless network or via a USB flash drive and, quite often, you can download applications from the App Store or the Internet.

However, there will be times when what you need is on a disc: a device driver, an application, data, and so on. One way to work around this problem is to attach an external DVD drive to one of the MacBook Air's USB ports. A good example is the MacBook Air SuperDrive, shown in Figure 2.3.

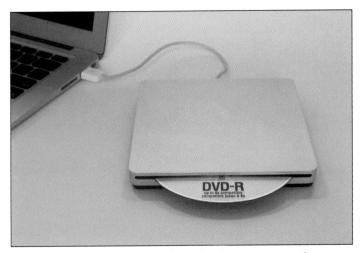

2.3 If a disc contains otherwise unobtainable data, you can attach a MacBook Air SuperDrive to the MacBook Air USB port.

**Note** The DVD or CD Sharing feature first appeared in Mac OS X 10.4.10. To share a DVD drive, the other Mac must be running at least that version of OS X. You can also share the optical drive on a Windows PC, as described in Chapter 11.

First, here are the necessary steps to share another Mac's DVD drive:

1. **In the Dock, click System Preferences.**
2. **Click Sharing.** The Sharing preferences appear.
3. **Select the DVD or CD Sharing check box.**
4. **If you want the user of the other Mac to be able to approve the remote use of the DVD drive (a good idea), leave the Ask me before allowing others to use my DVD drive check box selected.**

Now you're ready to use the remote DVD drive on MacBook Air. Follow these steps:

1. **On the other Mac, insert the disc that you want to access from MacBook Air.**
2. **On MacBook Air, click Finder in the Dock.**

**Note**   Remote DVD or CD Sharing doesn't work with most copyrighted discs, such as audio CDs and movie DVDs.

3. **In the sidebar's Devices section, click Remote Disc.** The Finder displays an icon for each Mac sharing a DVD drive, as shown in Figure 2.4.

2.4 In the sidebar's Devices section, click Remote Disc to see all of the Macs that are sharing their DVD drives.

4. **Double-click the icon for the Mac that has the disc you want to access.**

5. **If the remote Mac requires the user's permission to use the drive, click the Ask to use button.** The user on the remote Mac sees the dialog shown in Figure 2.5.

6. **The remote Mac user must click Accept at this point.** Finder displays an icon for the disc.

**2.5** The remote Mac user sees this dialog when you attempt to use that Mac's shared DVD drive.

7. **Double-click the disc icon.** Finder mounts the disc on the MacBook Air desktop, and you can now use the disc as though it was in a local drive.

# Exchanging Files Wirelessly with AirDrop

If you want to exchange a file between MacBook Air and another Mac, you have several ways to go about it:

- You could join both Macs to an existing infrastructure wireless network that uses a wireless router as the connection point.

- You could create and then join both Macs to an ad hoc wireless network that doesn't use a router.

- You could activate Bluetooth Sharing on both Macs, as described later in this chapter, and use the Bluetooth File Exchange utility.

All these methods work well enough, but they have their drawbacks. Infrastructure wireless networks require a router; ad hoc networks require (optionally, but importantly) the exchange of a network password; and Bluetooth file exchanges are fairly complicated to set up and can be quite slow.

None of these drawbacks is a deal-breaker in most situations, but you can easily think of times when a simple, fast way of sharing a file would be handy; for example, if you meet a friend at a coffee shop or a colleague at a conference. Wouldn't it be great if you could just somehow "beam" a file from your MacBook Air to the other person's Mac (and vice versa)?

I'm happy to report that this glorious day is now upon us. Mac OS X Lion introduces a new feature called AirDrop that looks for nearby AirDrop-friendly Macs and enables you to exchange files between the machines using a direct Wi-Fi link. There are no networks to join or create, there's nothing else to configure, and because it's Wi-Fi, the exchanges are lightning quick. Best of all, AirDrop uses a simple interface that shows icons for the other AirDrop-enabled Macs that are within range, and sending a file is as easy as dragging it from a Finder window and dropping it on the other Mac's icon (which then accepts or rejects the file).

The downside is that Apple has set up fairly rigid standards for which Macs support AirDrop. They must be running Lion, of course, but because these direct Wi-Fi links require special Wi-Fi hardware, only relatively recent Macs are capable of using AirDrop:

- **MacBook Air.** Late 2010 or newer
- **MacBook Pro.** Late 2008 or newer
- **MacBook.** Late 2008 or newer
- **iMac.** Early 2009 or newer
- **Mac Pro.** Early 2009 with AirPort Extreme card, or Mid 2010 or newer
- **Mac mini.** Mid 2010 or newer

How can you be sure whether a particular Mac supports AirDrop? Open Find and look in the Favorites section of the sidebar. If you don't see AirDrop, then your Mac doesn't have wireless hardware that passes muster for AirDrop.

If you do have two or more AirDrop-worthy Macs, here's how to exchange files between them:

1. **On your MacBook Air, open Finder and click AirDrop in the sidebar.**

2. **On the other Mac, the user must also open Finder and click AirDrop.** The AirDrop window displays icons for both Macs, as shown in Figure 2.6.

3. **Use a second Finder window to drag the file you want to exchange and drop it on the other Mac's AirDrop icon.** AirDrop asks the receiver to confirm the exchange.

**Caution** With the exchange complete, both users should now close the AirDrop window. This is a safety precaution, particularly in a public location, because it prevents other nearby AirDrop-enabled Macs from pestering you with file exchanges.

4. **The receiver of the file is given three choices.**

   - **Save & Open.** This choice saves the file to the Mac and then opens it in the corresponding application.

- **Save.** This choice saves the file to the Mac.

- **Decline.** This choice aborts the transfer.

2.6 The remote Mac user sees this dialog when you attempt to use that Mac's shared DVD drive.

# Transferring Settings Wirelessly from another Mac

Getting a new Mac is always a joyous event, but that joy is often short-lived when you realize that you need to transfer tons of settings, preferences, and files from your old Mac. Apple took pity on new Mac users when it released OS X 10.4 (Tiger), which included an application called Migration Assistant. This application automates the process of transferring user accounts, settings, files, and applications from one Mac to another. That's the good news.

The bad news was that Migration Assistant worked best over either a direct FireWire connection between the two Macs, or a wired network connection. This is bad news because, of course, MacBook Air doesn't include either a FireWire or Ethernet port for wired network connections. Fortunately, the bad news is only temporary because Apple has tweaked Migration Assistant to operate over a wireless connection (and the latest Macs can use a Thunderbolt connection for even faster transfers). This enables you to transfer settings to your MacBook Air from any Mac running Tiger or later.

**Caution**  If you'll be transferring data for a user account with the same name as yours (a likely scenario), you can run into conflicts during the transfer. To avoid this, log on to your MacBook Air using a different (administrator) user account, and then perform the transfer.

Here are the steps to follow:

1. **Shut down all your running applications.**

2. **On MacBook Air, choose Finder ⇨ Applications ⇨ Utilities ⇨ Migration Assistant.**
   The Migration Assistant appears.

3. **Select the From another Mac, PC, Time Machine backup, or other disk option and then click Continue.** Migration Assistant prompts you for your MacBook Air administrative password.

4. **Type your password and click OK.** The Select a Migration Method dialog appears.

5. **Select the From another Mac or PC option, and then click Continue.**

6. **On the other Mac, open Migration Assistant, select the To another Mac option, click Continue, type an administrative password for that Mac and click OK, and then click Continue.**

7. **Once MacBook Air locates the other Mac, click Continue.** Migration Assistant displays a passcode.

8. **Make sure the same passcode is also displayed on the other Mac, and then click Continue on both Macs.** The other Mac prepares the data for transfer and Migration Assistant on MacBook Air displays a list of items you can migrate, as shown in Figure 2.7.

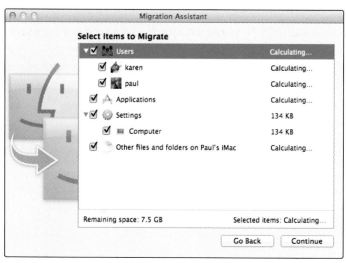

2.7 Use the Select Items to Migrate dialog to choose the data you want to transfer to MacBook Air.

9. **Select the check box beside each item you want to transfer.**

10. **Click Continue.** Migration Assistant transfers the data to MacBook Air.

11. **Click Quit on MacBook Air and on the other Mac.**

# Working with Bluetooth Devices

MacBook Air is already configured to use a wireless technology called Bluetooth. In the rest of this chapter, I cover what Bluetooth is; how to connect MacBook Air with various Bluetooth devices, such as a mouse, keyboard, and headset; and how to exchange files using MacBook Air's Bluetooth capabilities.

## A Bit of Bluetooth Background

You're probably familiar with Wi-Fi, the standard that enables you to perform networking chores without the usual network cables. Bluetooth is similar in that it enables you to exchange data between two devices without any kind of physical connection between them. Bluetooth uses radio frequencies to set up a communications link between the devices. That link is another example of an ad hoc wireless network (described earlier in this chapter), only in this case the network that Bluetooth creates is called a *piconet*.

Bluetooth is a short-distance networking technology with a maximum range of about 33 feet (10 meters). You can use MacBook Air's Bluetooth capabilities to make connections with a wide variety of devices, including the following:

- Bluetooth-enabled Mac
- Mouse (such as Apple's Wireless Mighty Mouse)
- Keyboard (such as Apple's Wireless Keyboard)
- Headset
- Cell phone
- Personal digital assistant
- Printer
- Digital camera

In theory, connecting Bluetooth devices should be criminally easy. You turn on each device's Bluetooth feature (in Bluetooth jargon, you make the devices discoverable), bring them within 33 feet of each other, and they connect without further ado. In practice, however, there's usually at least a bit of further ado (and sometimes plenty of it). This usually takes one or both of the following forms:

- **Making your device discoverable.** Unlike Wi-Fi devices that broadcast their signals constantly, most Bluetooth devices broadcast their availability only when you say so. This makes sense in many cases because you usually only want to use a Bluetooth device, such as a mouse or a keyboard, with a single computer. By controlling when the device is discoverable, you ensure that it works only with the computer you want it to.

- **Pairing MacBook Air and the device.** As a security precaution, many Bluetooth devices need to be paired with another device before the connection is established. In most cases, the pairing is accomplished by MacBook Air generating a multi-digit passkey that you must type into the Bluetooth device (assuming, of course, that it has some kind of keypad). In other cases, the device comes with a default passkey that you must enter into MacBook Air to set up the pairing. Finally, some devices set up an automatic pairing using an empty passkey.

## Connecting Bluetooth devices

Using a wireless device is a blissful state because, with no cord to tie you down, it gives you the freedom to interact with MacBook Air from just about anywhere. Wi-Fi devices are often cumbersome because they require a separate transceiver. These tend to be large and they also take up a USB port. However, because MacBook Air already has Bluetooth, you don't need anything else to use a Bluetooth-compatible device.

Follow these general steps to connect a Bluetooth mouse or keyboard:

1. **Click System Preferences in the Dock, and then click the Bluetooth icon.**

2. **Click Set Up New Device.** If you already have at least one Bluetooth device paired, click the + icon instead. The Bluetooth Setup Assistant appears and starts looking for nearby Bluetooth devices.

3. **Perform whatever steps are required to make your device discoverable.** Here are a couple of examples:

   - **Apple Magic Mouse, Magic Trackpad, or Mighty Mouse.** On the bottom of the mouse, slide the power switch off and then on again.

   - **Apple Wireless Keyboard.** Press the power button, which is on the top-right side of the keyboard.

4. **In the Devices list, click the device you want to pair, as shown in Figure 2.8.**

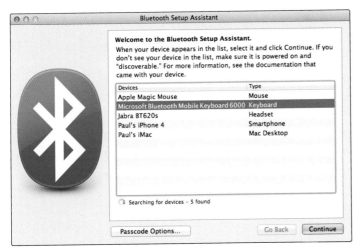

2.8 When the Bluetooth Setup Assistant discovers a Bluetooth device, it displays the device's name.

5. **Click Continue.** MacBook Air connects with the device. When MacBook Air connects with a device that requires a passkey for pairing, the Bluetooth Setup Assistant displays the passkey, as shown in Figure 2.9. Use the Bluetooth device to type the passkey. If the device is (or has) a keyboard, be sure to also press Return.

2.9 To establish a pairing between some Bluetooth devices, you must type a passkey on the device.

6. **Click Quit and your Bluetooth device is ready to use.**

**Note**

When MacBook Air wakes from sleep mode, the Bluetooth mouse doesn't always respond right away. Wait a few seconds (usually no more than about ten) to give the mouse time to reestablish its connection. Sometimes clicking the mouse helps it reconnect right away.

## Configuring a Bluetooth device

When you connect a Bluetooth device, in most cases you just go ahead and start using it. However, MacBook Air gives you a limited number of options for working with your Bluetooth device. For example, you can monitor the battery levels of many Bluetooth devices. To do this, click the Bluetooth status icon in the menu bar and then click the device. As you can see in Figure 2.10, the menu that appears includes an item that shows the current battery level. You can also use this menu to open the device's preferences or disconnect it.

**Note**

If you don't see the Bluetooth status icon, open System Preferences, click Bluetooth, and then select the Show Bluetooth status in the menu bar check box.

**2.10** Click the Bluetooth icon and then click the device to see its current battery level.

If you use multiple Bluetooth devices of the same type, the list of Bluetooth devices can get confusing because you don't have any direct way to tell one from another. To avoid this, you can often give your devices unique names (although not all Bluetooth devices support renaming). Here are the steps to rename a Bluetooth device:

1. **Click the Dock's System Preferences icon.** The System Preferences window appears.

2. **Click the Bluetooth icon.** The Bluetooth preferences appear, as shown in Figure 2.11, and you see a list of the Bluetooth devices currently paired. The status of these devices shows on the left as Connected. Those that were paired in the past show as Not Connected.

**2.11** The Bluetooth section of System Preferences displays a list of your Bluetooth devices.

3. **Click the device you want to rename.**

4. **Click the Actions button (the gear icon) and then click Rename.** System Preferences displays a text box.

5. **Type the new name and then click OK.** System Preferences updates the device's name. This name is stored on the device, so you see it even if you pair the device with another computer.

# Working with a Bluetooth headset

If you want to listen to music, headphones are a great way to go because the sound is often better than with the built-in MacBook Air speakers — and no one else is subjected to Led Zeppelin at top volume. Similarly, if you want to conduct a voice chat, a headset (a combination of headphones for listening and a microphone for talking) makes life easier because you don't need a separate microphone, and at least one half of your conversation remains private. Add Bluetooth to the mix, and you have an easy, wireless audio solution.

## Using Bluetooth headphones for sound output

When you connect Bluetooth headphones, MacBook Air doesn't automatically use them as the default sound output device. If you want to listen to, say, your iTunes library without disturbing your neighbors, you need to configure MacBook Air to use your headphones as the sound output device. Here's how:

1. **Click the System Preferences icon in the Dock.** The System Preferences window appears.

2. **Click the Sound icon.** The Sound preferences appear.

3. **Click the Output tab, and then select your Bluetooth headphones from the list, as shown in Figure 2.12.**

4. **Adjust the other sound settings as desired.**

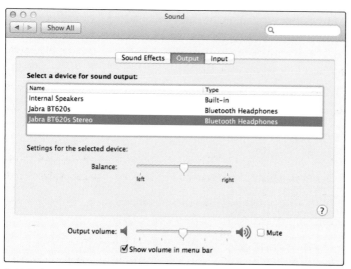

2.12 To keep your iTunes to yourself, select your Bluetooth headphones as MacBook Air's sound output device.

## Setting up a Bluetooth headset for voice chat

If you love to chat, typing messages back and forth is a fun way to pass the time. However, if you want to take things up a notch, you can use iChat's voice chat capabilities, which enable you to have voice conversations with your buddies. When you connect to a Bluetooth headset, MacBook Air usually sets up the headset as the voice chat microphone, but not as the sound output device. Follow these steps to configure voice chat to use your Bluetooth headset:

1. **Click the Dock's iChat icon and choose iChat ⇨ Preferences from the menu that appears.**

2. **Click the Audio/Video tab.**

3. **Select your Bluetooth headset from the Microphone and Sound output lists.**

**Genius** If your buddies often tell you to stop shouting in voice chat, even though you're using your normal voice, you'll need to make a quick volume adjustment. In the Audio chat window, you can click and drag the volume slider to the left. To set the global volume level, choose System Preferences ⇨ Sound and then click the Input tab. Click and drag the Input volume slider to the left to reduce the volume.

# Exchanging Files Using Bluetooth

If you have a Bluetooth device that works with document, music, and image files, or data such as appointments and addresses, you can exchange files between MacBook Air and the Bluetooth device. However, bear in mind that this is useful only for small files. Bluetooth isn't the fastest technology out there, so these transfers can be glacially slow. Small items, such as addresses and appointments, transfer reasonably fast, but it can take a few minutes to transfer a single MP3 file. Still, if you have no other way to transfer data, Bluetooth will do in a pinch.

To transfer files from MacBook Air to a Bluetooth device, you can use MacBook Air's Bluetooth File Exchange utility. To transfer files from a Bluetooth device to MacBook Air, you can activate and configure MacBook Air's Bluetooth Sharing feature.

## Making sure MacBook Air is discoverable

If you want other Bluetooth devices to see MacBook Air and initiate pairings or other operations, such as cell phone remote control, you need to make sure not only that MacBook Air's Bluetooth power is on, but also that MacBook Air is discoverable. Follow these steps:

1. **Click the Bluetooth status icon in the menu bar, and then choose Open Bluetooth Preferences.**

2. **Select the Bluetooth Power check box.**

3. **Select the Discoverable check box.**

## Browsing a Bluetooth device

When you browse a Bluetooth device, you examine the contents of the device and, optionally, get one or more files from the device. You can do this by using the Bluetooth File Exchange utility. To browse a device, follow these steps:

1. **In Finder, choose Applications ⇨ Utilities ⇨ Bluetooth File Exchange.** If you see the Select File to Send dialog, click Cancel.

2. **Choose File ⇨ Browse Device.** You can also press Shift+⌘+O. The Browse Device dialog appears and displays a list of available Bluetooth devices.

3. **Click the device you want to browse.**

4. **Click Browse.** The Browsing dialog appears.

5. **Pair your Mac and the Bluetooth device.**

   - In some cases, the Bluetooth device generates or asks you to enter a passcode, and your Mac then prompts you for the passcode, as shown in Figure 2.13. Type the passcode and click Pair.

   - Other Bluetooth devices require only simple permission for pairing. Click Allow to initiate the pairing.

**2.13** You see this dialog if the Bluetooth device generates a pairing passcode.

6. **In the Browsing dialog that appears, double-click the folders to get to the one you want to view.** If you want to download a file to MacBook Air, double-click the file, select a location, and then click Save.

## Sending files to a Bluetooth device

If you have some data you want to share with a Bluetooth device, the Bluetooth File Exchange utility is only too happy to help you do it. Here's how it works:

1. **In Finder, choose Applications ⇨ Utilities ⇨ Bluetooth File Exchange.** If you don't see the Select File to Send dialog right away, choose File ⇨ Send File. You can also press ⌘+O.

2. **Choose the file you want to upload, and then click Send.** The Select Bluetooth Device dialog appears and displays a list of waiting devices.

3. **Click the device you want to use.**

4. **Click Send.** The Bluetooth File Exchange attempts to connect with the device. Use the device interface to accept the incoming file.

# Activating Bluetooth sharing

The Bluetooth File Exchange utility is great for browsing and sending stuff to a Bluetooth device or to another Bluetoothed Mac, but what about the other way around? That is, what about getting a Bluetooth device to send things to MacBook Air? If the Bluetooth device is another Mac then, of course, you can crank up Bluetooth File Exchange on that computer and use the techniques from the preceding two sections in this chapter. For cell phones, PDAs, and other file-friendly devices, connect them to MacBook Air and initiate the browsing or sending from there.

To do this, you must activate and configure MacBook Air's Bluetooth Sharing feature. This feature enables other Bluetooth devices to connect to MacBook Air, specifies what those devices can see and do, and determines whether pairing is required to browse or send files to MacBook Air.

Here are the steps required to activate and configure Bluetooth Sharing:

1.  **Click the Dock's System Preferences icon, and then click Sharing.**

2.  **Select the Bluetooth Sharing check box to turn on the Bluetooth Sharing feature, as shown in Figure 2.14.**

2.14 Select the Bluetooth Sharing check box and then use the other controls to configure this feature.

3. **Configure MacBook Air to receive files.**

   - **When receiving items.** Use this list to determine what MacBook Air does when a Bluetooth device attempts to send a file. It's usually best to choose Ask What to Do so you always have control over the transfer. If you never want files sent to MacBook Air, choose Never Allow instead.

   - **Folder for accepted items.** Use this list to choose the folder where files sent to MacBook Air are stored.

4. **Configure MacBook Air for browsing.**

   - **When other devices browse.** Use this list to determine what MacBook Air does when a Bluetooth device attempts to browse the Mac's file. Again, it's best to choose Ask What to Do so you always have control over the browsing. If browsing isn't a problem for you, you can avoid being pestered by choosing Always Allow instead. If you never want Bluetooth devices to browse MacBook Air, choose Never Allow.

   - **Folder others can browse.** Use this list to choose the folder that Bluetooth devices can browse.

# How Do I Synchronize MacBook Air with Other Devices?

MacBook Air is a big part of your life, but it's not your whole life. You have music, photos, podcasts, calendars, and addresses on your iPod, iPhone, or iPad, and you have files, bookmarks, mail accounts, calendars, contacts, and more on your iCloud account. That's a lot to keep track of, so how do you keep up? The secret is synchronization: ensuring that the data on MacBook Air is the same as the data on your other devices. Fortunately, MacBook Air has some great tools that make it easy to keep MacBook Air and your life in sync.

# Synchronizing with an iPod, iPad, or iPhone

Long gone are the days when the only thing you could use to fill up your portable media player was music. With modern iPods, iPads, iPhones, and the latest version of iTunes, you can cram your players not only with your favorite tunes, but also with music videos, audiobooks, movies, TV shows, eBooks, podcasts, photos, contacts, calendars, and even games. Suddenly those once massive multigigabyte hard drives don't look so big anymore. Whatever your device's hard drive size, if you find yourself running out of space, the alternative isn't (necessarily) to go out and buy a bigger player. Instead, iTunes gives you many options for controlling what gets added to (or removed from) your iPod, iPad, or iPhone when you synchronize it.

**Genius**  If iTunes doesn't fire up automatically when you connect your device, you can force it to do so. In iTunes, click your iPod, iPad, or iPhone in the Devices list, click the Summary tab, and then select the Open iTunes when this *device* is connected check box, where *device* is iPod, iPad, or iPhone. Click Apply to put the setting into effect.

## Synchronizing music and videos

An iOS device — whether it's an iPod, iPad, or iPhone — is a digital music player, so you probably load up yours with a lot of audio content. Depending on the type of iOS device you have, you may have a lot of music videos stored on it, as well. To get the most out of an iOS device's music and video capabilities, you need to know all the ways you can synchronize these items. For example, if you'll be using your device primarily as a music player and it has far more hard drive capacity than you need for all your digital audio, feel free to throw all your music onto the player. On the other hand, you may use your iOS device for other things, so you may want only certain songs and videos on the player to make it easier to navigate. In such cases, you need to configure the device to synchronize only those songs and videos you want to play.

You can easily tell iTunes to toss every last song and video onto your device, or just selected playlists, artists, albums, or music genres. Follow these steps:

1. **In iTunes, click your iPod, iPad, or iPhone in the Devices list.**
2. **Click the Music tab.**

3. **Select the Sync Music check box.** From this point, the options you select determine what actually synchronizes.

- **Select the Selected playlists, artists, albums, and genres option to choose specific playlists to be included, as shown in Figure 3.1.** If any of the selected playlists contain videos you do not want synchronized, deselect the Include music videos check box.

- **Select the Include music videos check box to include all music videos.**

- **For your iPhone or iPad, select the Include voice memos check box to include any voice recordings you've made.**

- **Select the Automatically fill free space with songs check box to tell iTunes to fill up any remaining free space on your device with a selection of related music from your library.**

4. **Click Apply.** iTunes syncs the device using the new settings.

3.1 Select the Selected playlists, artists, albums, and genres option, and then use the lists to select the items you want to synchronize.

If you want to control the individual tracks that get synced to your iPod, you can manage your music and videos by hand. One way to do this is to use the check boxes that appear beside each track in your iTunes Music library.

Here's how you do it:

1. **In the Devices list, click your iPod, iPad, or iPhone.**

2. **Click the Summary tab.**

3. **Select the Sync only checked songs and videos check box.**

4. **Click Apply.** If iTunes starts synchronizing your device, click the Cancel button, as shown in Figure 3.2.

5. **In the Library list, click Music.** If a track's check box is selected, iTunes synchronizes it with your device. If a track's check box is deselected, iTunes doesn't sync it with your device; if the track is already on your device, iTunes removes the track.

Unchecked tracks don't          Click here to cancel
get synced                      a sync in progress

3.2 When you configure your device to synchronize only checked songs and videos, deselect the check box for each track you don't want synced.

6. **Click your iPod, iPad, or iPhone in the Devices list.**

7. **Click the Summary tab.**

8. **Click Sync.** iTunes synchronizes only the selected tracks.

An alternative method is to drag tracks from the Music library and drop them on your device. Here's how this works:

1. **In the Devices list, click your iPod, iPad, or iPhone.**

2. **Click the Summary tab and select the Manually manage music and videos check box.** iTunes asks you to confirm.

3. **Click OK, click Apply, and then click Music.**

4. **Select the tracks you want to sync.** For noncontiguous tracks, ⌘+click each track. For contiguous groups, Shift+click the first track, hold down Shift, and then click the last track.

**Genius**

For maximum control over manual synchronizing, you can configure your device to sync checked tracks, and tracks that you drag and drop. In the Summary tab, select the Sync only checked songs and videos check box before you select the Manually manage music and videos check box.

5. **Click and drag the selected tracks to the device icon that appears in the Devices list and drop the selected tracks on the device icon.** iTunes syncs the selected tracks.

# Synchronizing movies

It wasn't all that long ago when technology prognosticators and pundits laughed at the idea of people watching movies on a 2.5-inch screen. Who could stand to watch even a music video on such a tiny screen? The pundits were wrong, of course, because nowadays it's not unusual for people to watch not only music videos, but also short films, animated shorts, and even full-length movies on their iPods and iPhones. Of course, watching movies and videos on the gorgeous — and relatively large — iPad screen is a no-brainer.

The major problem with synchronizing movies is that their file sizes tend to be quite large — even short films lasting just a few minutes weigh in at dozens of megabytes, and full-length movies are several gigabytes. Clearly, there's a compelling need to manage your movies to avoid filling up your device and leaving no room for your favorite band's latest album. If you have an iPad, iPhone, or video-friendly iPod, follow the steps in the next two sections to configure and run the movie synchronization.

## Synchronizing rented movies

If you've rented a movie from iTunes, you can move that movie to your device and watch it there. Note that you're *moving* the rented movie, not copying it. You can store rented movies in only one location at a time, so if you synchronize the movie to your device, it's no longer available on your computer.

Follow these steps to sync a rented movie to your device:

1. **In iTunes, click your iPod, iPad, or iPhone in the Devices list.**

2. **Click the Movies tab.**

3. **In the Rented Movies section, shown in Figure 3.3, click the Move button beside the rented movie you want to shift to your device.** iTunes adds the movie to the On *"device"* list (where *device* is the name of your iPod, iPad, or iPhone).

4. **Click Apply.** iTunes syncs the device using your new rented movie settings.

3.3 In the Rented Movies section of the Movies tab, click Move to transfer a rented movie to your iPod, iPad, or iPhone.

## Synchronizing purchased or downloaded movies

If you've purchased a movie from iTunes or added a video to your iTunes library, follow these steps to synchronize some, or all of them, to your iPod, iPad, or iPhone:

1. **In iTunes, click your device in the Devices list.**

2. **Click the Movies tab.**

3. **Select the Sync Movies check box.**

4. **If you want iTunes to choose some of the movies automatically, select the Automatically include check box and proceed to Step 5.** If you prefer to choose all the movies manually, deselect the Automatically include check box and skip to Step 6.

**Note**

A movie is unwatched if you haven't yet viewed it, either in iTunes or on your device. If you watch it on your device, the player sends this information to iTunes when you next synchronize. This is one of the rare examples of information that gets sent to iTunes when you synchronize a device.

5. **Choose an option from the pop-up menu:**

   - **All.** Choose this item to sync every movie.

   - **X Most Recent.** Choose this item to sync the X (that is, the number of) most recent movies you've added to iTunes (where "most recent" refers to the date you downloaded the movie, not the movie's release date).

   - **All Unwatched.** Choose this item to sync all the movies you haven't yet played.

   - **X Most Recent Unwatched.** Choose this item to sync the X most recent movies you haven't yet played.

   - **X Least Recent Unwatched.** Choose this item to sync the X oldest movies you haven't yet played (where "oldest" refers to the date you downloaded the movie).

**Genius**

If you watch a movie, but want to leave it on the device during the next sync, you need to mark it as new (that is, unwatched). In iTunes, choose the Movies library, right-click the movie, and then choose Mark as New.

6. **Select the check box beside any other movie you want to synchronize, as shown in Figure 3.4.**

7. **Click Apply.** iTunes syncs the iPod using your new movie settings.

**Genius**

If you download a music video from the web and then import it into iTunes (by choosing File ⇨ Import), iTunes adds the video to its Movies library. To display it in the Music library instead, open the Movies library, right-click the music video, and then click Get Info. Click the Video tab, use the Kind list to choose Music Video, then click OK. iTunes moves the music video to the Music folder.

3.4 In the Movies tab, select Sync Movies and choose the films you want to synchronize.

# Synchronizing TV show episodes

If the average video device is at risk of being filled up by a few large movie files, the risk is probably even greater that the device could become overwhelmed by a large number of TV show episodes. A single half-hour episode eats up approximately 250MB, so even a modest collection of shows consumes multiple gigabytes of precious device hard drive space.

This means that it's crucial to monitor your collection of TV show episodes and keep your device synchronized with only the episodes you need. Fortunately, iTunes gives you a decent set of tools to handle this:

1. **In iTunes, click your device in the Devices list.**

2. **Click the TV Shows tab.**

3. **Select the Sync TV Shows check box.**

4. **If you want iTunes to choose some of the episodes automatically, select the Automatically include check box and proceed to Steps 5 and 6.** If you prefer to choose all the episodes manually, deselect the Automatically include check box and skip to Step 7.

5. **Choose an option from the drop-down menu.**

   - **All.** Choose this item to sync every TV show episode.

   - **X Most Recent.** Choose this item to sync the *X* (that is, the number of) most recent episodes (where "most recent" refers to the date you downloaded the episode, not the episode's release date).

- **All Unwatched.** Choose this item to sync all episodes you haven't yet viewed.

- **X Most Recent Unwatched.** Choose this item to sync the X most recent episodes you haven't yet viewed.

- **X Least Recent Unwatched.** Choose this item to sync the X oldest episodes you haven't yet viewed (where "oldest" refers to the date you downloaded the episode).

**Note** As with movies, a TV episode is unwatched if you haven't yet viewed it either in iTunes or on your device. If you watch an episode on your device, the player sends this information to iTunes when you next synchronize.

6. **Choose an option from the second pop-up menu:**

- **All shows.** Select this option to apply the choice from Step 5 to all of your TV shows.

- **Selected shows.** Select this option to apply the choice from Step 5 to only the TV shows you select, as shown in Figure 3.5.

7. **Click Apply.** iTunes synchronizes the device using your new TV show settings.

**Genius** In iTunes, to mark a TV episode as unwatched choose the TV Shows library, right-click the episode, and then choose Mark as New.

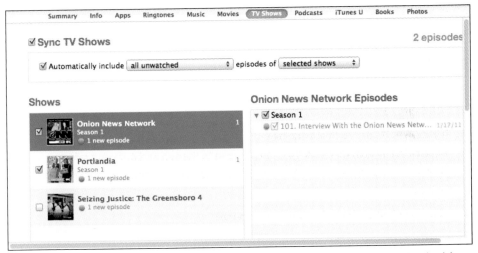

3.5 To synchronize specific TV shows, select the selected shows option and then select the check boxes for each show you want synced.

# Synchronizing podcasts

In many ways, podcasts are the most problematic of the various media you can synchronize with your device. Not that podcasts themselves pose any concern. Quite the contrary — they're so addictive that collecting them by the dozens is not unusual. Why is that a problem? Most professional podcasts are at least a few megabytes in size, and many are tens of megabytes. A large-enough collection can put a serious dent in your device's remaining storage space.

All the more reason to take control of the podcast syncing process. Here's how you do it:

1. **In iTunes, click your device in the Devices list.**

2. **Click the Podcasts tab.**

3. **Select the Sync Podcasts check box.**

4. **If you want iTunes to choose some of the podcasts automatically, select the Automatically include check box and proceed to Steps 5 and 6.** If you prefer to choose all the podcasts manually, deselect the Automatically include check box and skip to Step 7.

**Note**   A podcast episode is unplayed if you haven't yet played at least part of the episode, either in iTunes or on your device. If you play an episode on your device, the player sends this information to iTunes when you next synchronize. Even better, your device also lets iTunes know if you paused in the middle of an episode; when you play that episode in iTunes, it starts at the point where you left off.

5. **Choose a sync option from the first pop-up menu:**

   - **All.** Choose this item to synchronize every podcast.

   - **X Most Recent.** Choose this item to synchronize the X (that is, the number of) most recent podcasts (where "most recent" refers to the date you downloaded the podcast, not the podcast's release date).

   - **All Unplayed.** Choose this item to synchronize all the podcasts you haven't yet played.

   - **X Most Recent Unplayed.** Choose this item to synchronize the X most recent podcasts that you haven't yet played.

   - **X Least Recent Unplayed.** Choose this item to synchronize the X oldest podcasts that you haven't yet played (where "oldest" refers to the date you downloaded the podcast).

- **All New.** Choose this item to synchronize all podcasts published since the last sync.

- **X Most Recent New.** Choose this item to synchronize the X most recent podcasts published since the last sync.

- **X Least Recent New.** Choose this item to synchronize the X oldest podcasts published since the last sync.

6. **Choose an option from the second pop-up menu:**

- **All podcasts.** Select this option to apply the option from Step 4 to all of your podcasts.

- **Selected podcasts.** Select this option to apply the option from Step 4 to only the podcasts you select, as shown in Figure 3.6.

**Genius**

To mark a podcast episode as unplayed, in iTunes choose the Podcasts library, right-click the episode, and then choose Mark as New.

7. **Click Apply.** iTunes synchronizes the iPod using your new podcast settings.

3.6 To synchronize specific podcasts, choose the selected podcasts option and then select the check boxes for each podcast you want to synchronize.

# Synchronizing photos

If your device can display photos (and all new iPods, iPads, and iPhones can), you can use iTunes to synchronize photos between your device and either your Pictures folder or iPhoto. Note that Apple supports a number of image file types — the usual TIFF and JPEG formats that you normally use for photos, as well as BMP, GIF, JPG2000 or JP2, PICT, PNG, PSD, and SGI.

If you use MacBook Air to process a lot of photos and you want copies of some, or all of them, on your device, follow these steps to synchronize them:

1. **In iTunes, click your device in the Devices list.**

2. **Click the Photos tab.**

3. **Select the Sync Photos from check box and choose an option from the drop-down menu.** In the Sync Photos from list, you have three choices:

    - **Pictures.** Choose this item to sync the images in your Pictures folder.

    - **Choose folder.** Choose this command to sync the images contained in another folder.

    - **iPhoto.** Choose this item to sync the photos, albums, and events you've set up in iPhoto.

4. **Select the photos you want to synchronize.** The controls you see depend on what you chose in Step 3:

    - **If you chose either Pictures or Choose folder.** In this case, select either the All photos option or the Selected folders option. If you select the latter, select the check box beside each subfolder you want to synchronize, as shown in Figure 3.7.

    - **If you chose iPhoto.** In this case, you get two further options: Select the All Photos, Albums, and Faces option to synchronize your entire iPhoto library; select the Selected Albums, Events, and Faces option to select the check box beside each album, event, and face you want to synchronize.

5. **If you selected either the Selected folders option or the Selected albums option, click and drag the folders or albums to set the order you prefer.**

6. **Click Apply.** iTunes synchronizes the device using your new photo settings.

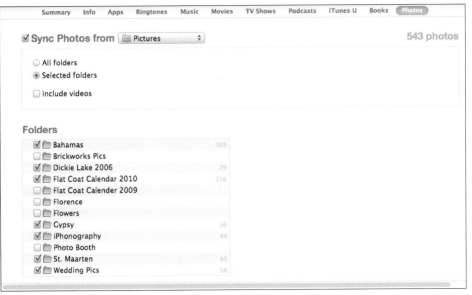

**3.7** To synchronize photos from specific folders, choose the Selected folders option, and then select the check box for each folder you want to sync.

**Note**

iTunes doesn't synchronize exact copies of your photos to the device. Instead, it creates what Apple calls TV-quality versions of each image. These are copies of the images that have been reduced in size to match that of the device's screen. This not only makes the synchronizing process faster, but it also means that the photos take up much less room on your device.

## Synchronizing contacts

Although you can certainly add contacts directly on your iPad, iPhone, or iPod touch, adding, editing, grouping, and deleting contacts is a lot easier on your MacBook Air (and it's a must if you're dealing with a regular iPod which, yes, does come with a Contacts feature). So a good way to approach contacts is to manage them using MacBook Air's Address Book application and then synchronize your contacts with your device.

Follow these steps to synchronize contacts with your iPad, iPhone, or iPod touch:

1. **In iTunes, click your device in the Devices list.**

2. **Click the Info tab.**

3. **Select the Sync Address Book Contacts check box and select an option.**

● **All contacts.** Select this option to synchronize all your Address Book contacts.

● **Selected groups.** Select this option to synchronize only the groups you pick. In the group list, select the check box beside each group that you want synchronized, as shown in Figure 3.8.

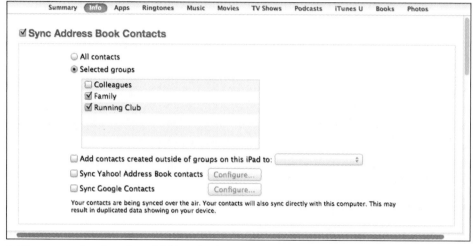

3.8 You can synchronize selected Address Book contact groups with your device.

4. **If you want to make the sync a two-way street, select the Add contacts created outside of groups on this device to check box, and then choose a group from the menu.**

5. **If you have a Yahoo! account, and you also want your Yahoo! Address Book contacts synced, select the Sync Yahoo! Address Book contacts check box, type your Yahoo! ID and password, and click OK.**

6. **If you have a Google account and you also want your Google Contacts synced, select the Sync Google Contacts check box, type your Google account email address and password, and click OK.**

7. **Click Apply.** iTunes synchronizes the device using your new contacts settings.

Follow these steps to sync contacts with your iPod:

1. **In iTunes, click your iPod in the Devices list.**

2. **Click the Info tab.**

3. **Select the Sync Address Book Contacts check box and select an option.**

   - **All contacts.** Select this option to synchronize all your Address Book contacts.

   - **Selected groups.** Select this option to synchronize only the groups you pick. In the group list, select the check box beside each group that you want synchronized.

4. **Select the Include contacts' photos check box if you have photos for some, or all of your contacts.**

5. **Click Apply.** iTunes synchronizes the iPod using your new contacts settings.

# Synchronizing calendars

Like contacts, you can also use your iPad, iPhone, or iPod touch to create events and perform other calendar maintenance. However, most people find it a bit easier to manage their schedule using iCal on their Mac (although the Calendar app on the iPad is awfully good). And, certainly, you must use iCal if you want to add your events to your iPod's Calendar feature.

Follow these steps to synchronize calendars with your device:

1. **In iTunes, click your device in the Devices list.**

2. **For an iPad, iPhone, or iPod touch, click the Info tab.** For an iPod, click the Contacts tab.

3. **Select the Sync iCal Calendars check box.**

4. **Select an option to add the calendar data as well.** If you want to bypass synchronizing calendars, deselect the Sync iCal Calendars check box and click Apply.

   - **All calendars.** Select this option to sync all your iCal calendars.

   - **Selected calendars.** Select this option to sync only the calendars you pick. In the calendar list, select the check box beside each calendar that you want to synchronize, as shown in Figure 3.9.

5. **For iPad, iPhone, and iPod touch, to control how far back the calendar synchronization goes, select the Do not sync events older than X days check box (where X is the number of days of calendar history you want included in the synchronization).** Then type the number of days of calendar history you want to see on your device.

6. **Click Apply.** iTunes synchronizes the device using your new calendar settings.

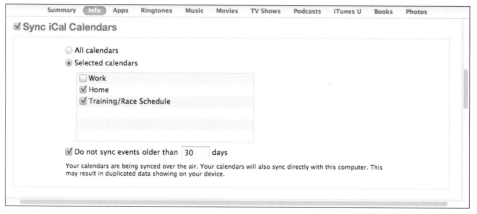

3.9 You can synchronize selected calendars with your device.

# Synchronizing apps

Many people use their iPad, iPhone, or iPod touch to download apps, but you can also use iTunes to get what you need from the App Store. After you download an app or two into iTunes, they won't do you much good just sitting there. To actually use the apps, you need to get them on your device. Similarly, if you've grabbed an app or three on your device, it's a good idea to back them up on your computer.

You can accomplish both goals by synchronizing apps between your computer and your iPad, iPhone, or iPod touch:

1. **In iTunes, click your iPad, iPhone, or iPod touch in the Devices list.**

2. **Click the Apps tab.**

3. **Select the Sync Apps check box.**

4. **In the app list, select the check box beside each app that you want to sync, as shown in Figure 3.10.**

5. **To arrange your app icons on your device, click a Home page thumbnail to display its icons, then click and drag the icons.** You can drag them within the current page, to a different page, or one on top of another to create an app folder.

6. **Click Apply.** iTunes synchronizes the device using your new app settings.

3.10 You can synchronize selected apps with your iPad, iPhone, or iPod touch.

# Synchronizing eBooks

If you've used your computer to grab an eBook from the iBookstore, or have added an eBook to the iTunes library, you'll want to get it onto your iPad, iPhone, or iPod touch as soon as possible. Similarly, if you've downloaded a few eBooks on your device, it's a good idea to back them up on your computer.

You can do both by synchronizing eBooks between your computer and your device:

1. **In iTunes, click your device in the Devices list.**

2. **Click the Books tab.**

3. **Select the Sync Books check box.**

4. **In the book list, select the check box beside each book that you want to sync, as shown in Figure 3.11.**

5. **Click Apply.** iTunes synchronizes the device using your new book settings.

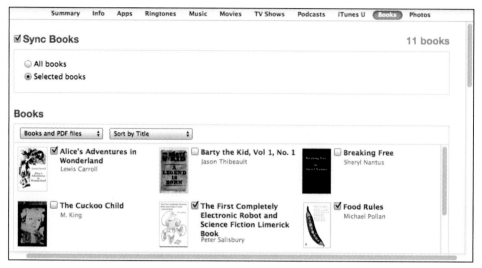

3.11 You can sync selected eBooks with your iPad, iPhone, or iPod touch.

## Synchronizing games

Listening to tunes on your iPod is a great way to pass the time, but sometimes you need more to keep yourself occupied. If you find yourself in a long lineup or otherwise delayed without a book in sight, perhaps a rousing game of Tetris would interest you. Fortunately, that's a lot easier to do now that the iTunes Store is selling quite a few games designed for the iPod screen. You can get Tetris and other old favorites, such as Pac-Man, Sonic the Hedgehog, Solitaire, and Mahjong, as well as newer pastimes, like Sudoku, Lost, and Brain Challenge.

Once you purchase a game or three from the iTunes Store, follow these steps to synchronize them to your iPod:

1. **In iTunes, click your iPod in the Devices list.**

2. **Click the Games tab.**

3. **Select the Sync Games check box.**

4. **In the games list, select the check box beside each game that you want to sync, as shown in Figure 3.12.**

5. **Click Apply.** iTunes syncs the iPod using your new games settings.

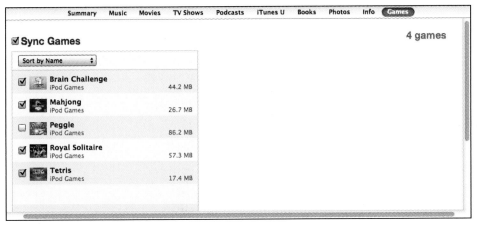

3.12 You can synchronize games with your iPod.

# Synchronizing with iCloud

If you need to transfer important data back and forth between MacBook Air and your iCloud account, the iCloud synchronization feature is for you. You can synchronize some or all of the following items:

- **Bookmarks.** The bookmarks you've saved in Safari.

- **Calendars.** Your iCal calendars, including all of your events and to-do items.

- **Contacts.** Your Address Book contacts.

- **Documents and data.** The documents and other data that you create with apps. As I write this, document sync works only with the iWork applications, but expect to see lots of third-party apps supporting document syncing in the near future.

- **Mail accounts.** The details of the email accounts you've set up in Mail.

- **Notes.** The notes that you've created in Mail.

- **Photo Stream.** The photos you've taken with your iPhone, iPod touch, or iPad. iCloud stores your most recent 30 days' worth of photos, or up to 1,000 shots in all, and syncs those photos with all your iOS devices as well as MacBook Air.

**Note**

Photo Stream isn't just about new photos that you take with your iOS device.

Why synchronize? Because it quickly becomes tiresome and inefficient to store multiple copies of your digital stuff on multiple digital devices. Why maintain separate collections of bookmarks on your MacBook Air, your iPhone, and your iPad, when with iCloud you can maintain a single bookmark collection and have it synced to all your devices automatically? Beats me! Another good reason to synchronize is to get access to items over the web, such as your contacts, calendars, and mail accounts. By logging on to your iCloud account, you can use the iCloud web apps to access your data from any location, using any computer.

**Note**

If you have an iCloud account, I cover a lot of great things you can do with it in Chapter 5.

You have to configure MacBook Air to specify what information you want synchronized with your iCloud account. Follow these steps to set your preferences:

1. **Click the System Preferences icon in the Dock.** The System Preferences application appears.

2. **In the Internet & Wireless section, click iCloud.** System Preferences displays a list of the items you can sync with iCloud.

3. **Select the check box beside each data item you want to synchronize with your iCloud account.** In most cases you see "Starting" to the right of the item (see Figure 3.13), which tells you that System Preferences is setting up the synchronization for that item.

To keep your MacBook Air in sync with an iOS device, you first need to add your iCloud account to your device. On the iOS device Home screen, tap Settings, tap iCloud, and then use the On/Off switches (see Figure 3.14) to specify which types of data you want iCloud to sync between your device and your MacBook Air.

3.13 When you see "Starting" after you select a check box, it means System Preferences is configuring the sync for that item.

3.14 On your iOS device, such as an iPad shown here, open the Settings app and tap iCloud to choose which data items you want to sync.

# How Do I Use MacBook Air to Organize My Real Life?

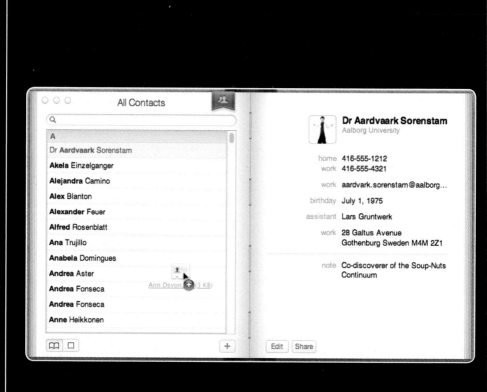

MacBook Air has never been only about the technology. It looks stylish, and it just works. As a result, many MacBook Air users don't know or care about things like the speed of the machine's CPU or even how much memory they have installed. These things don't matter all that much because MacBook Air has always been about helping you get things done, and helping you make your life better, more creative, and more efficient. As you see in this chapter, MacBook Air can also help make your life — particularly your contacts, appointments, and to-do lists — more organized.

# Managing Your Contacts

One of the paradoxes of modern life is that as your contact information becomes more important, you store less and less of that information in the easiest database system of them all — your memory. That is, instead of memorizing phone numbers like you used to, you now store your contact info electronically. When you think about it, this isn't exactly surprising because it's not just a landline number that you have to remember for each person anymore. It might also be a cell number, an instant-message handle, an email address, a website, a Twitter username, as well as a physical address.

That's a lot to remember, so it makes sense to go the electronic route. For most Mac users, "electronic" means the Address Book application. Initially, this app seems basic enough, but it's actually loaded with useful features that can help you organize and get the most out of the contact-management side of your life.

## Saving a person's contact information

Entering a person's contact data by hand into a new Address Book card is tedious at the best of times, so it helps if you can find a faster way to do it. For example, if you can cajole a contact into sending his or her contact data electronically, you can add that data with just a couple of mouse moves.

What do I mean when I talk about sending contact data electronically? Long ago, the world's contact-management gurus came up with a standard file format for contact data: the vCard. It's a kind of digital business card that exists as a separate file. People can pass this data along by attaching their (or someone else's) card to an email message. (You'll learn how to do this with your own contact data in the next section.)

If you get a message with contact data, you see an icon for the VCF file, as shown in Figure 4.1.

You now have two ways to get this data into your Address Book:

- **In most cases you can simply double-click the vCard file icon.** If this doesn't work, right-click the vCard file icon, and then choose Open With ⇨ Address Book.
- **Click Address Book in the Dock.** Click and drag the vCard file icon, then drop it inside the Address Book window, as shown in Figure 4.2. If Address Book isn't running, you can automatically launch it by dragging the vCard icon and dropping it on the Address Book icon in the Dock.

When Address Book asks you to confirm the new card, click Add.

From: **Paul Sellars**                                    Hide
Subject: Ann's contact info
Date: August 8, 2011 5:12:28 PM EDT
To: Paul McFedries

1 Attachment, 3 KB    Save ▼    Quick Look

Hi Paul,

As requested, Ann Devon's contact information is in the attached file.

Cheers,
Paul

Ann Devon.vcf (3 KB)

4.1 If you get a message with an attached vCard, an icon for the file appears
in the message.

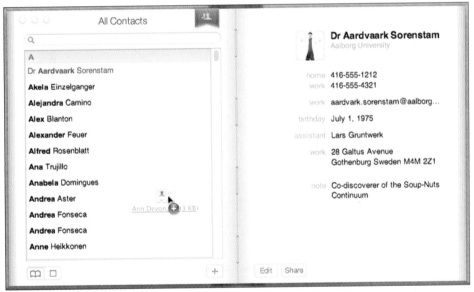

4.2 You can click and drag the vCard attachment and drop it inside the Address Book window.

# Sending your contact information

As you saw in the previous section, the easiest way to get someone's contact info into your Address
Book is to use that person's vCard, which is typically sent to you as an email attachment. So why

not turn things around and offer the same convenience to your colleagues, friends, and family? Create your own vCard and fire it off to whoever you think wants it.

A card should have been added automatically when you set up your user account, so look for it under your username. If for some reason you don't have a card, choose File ⇨ New Card, or press ⌘+N and fill in the fields. Make sure that Address Book knows this is your card by choosing it and then selecting Card ⇨ Make This My Card. This changes the standard card icon to a silhouette of a head shot and also adds "me" to your picture, as shown in Figure 4.3.

**Genius**

One of the main advantages to designating your own card is that you can easily navigate to it by choosing Address Book's Card ⇨ Go to My Card command.

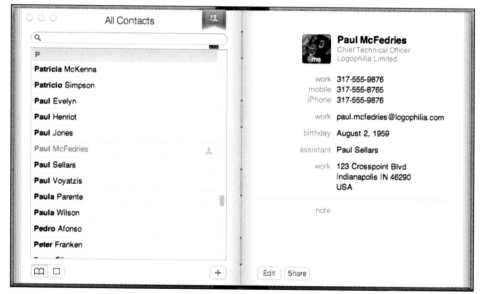

4.3 When you specify a card as your own, Address Book changes the icon that appears to the right of your name to the silhouette of a head shot.

**Genius**

Before sending your card, note that Address Book includes your card's picture by default. If you don't want to add your picture to your vCard, choose Address Book ⇨ Preferences, click the vCard tab, and then deselect the Export photos in vCards check box.

Now you're ready to create your own vCard. Follow these steps:

1. **In Address Book, choose your card and then click Edit.**

2. **Make sure your Address Book card contains all the data you want to include in your vCard and that it is accurate.**

3. **If there are any items you don't want to include in your vCard, deselect the check to the right of each item.**

4. **Click Done.**

5. **Click Share.** Address Book creates a vCard file for your card and attaches it to a new email message.

6. **Fill in the rest of the message (recipient, subject, and so on), and then click Send.**

**Genius**

Some corporate mail servers may block vCard attachments because of security concerns, so your attachment might not make it through. If that happens, create a separate vCard file by choosing your card and then choosing File ➪ Export ➪ Export vCard. Now compress the vCard file into a Zip file (right-click the file and then click Compress) and send the Zip file as an attachment to get it through the corporate firewall. Your recipient can then extract the vCard file from the Zip archive.

## Sending messages to a group of contacts

Choosing recipients one by one is fine if your list of recipients changes each time, or if you email only a particular collection of recipients every once in a while. However, these days it's fairly common to send messages to the same bunch of recipients frequently. It could be the other people in your department, colleagues on a particular project, your family members, your rocketry club members, or whoever. In each case, selecting all those addresses one at a time gets old quickly. Fortunately, the Address Book can help you eliminate the drudgery of addressing these messages. How? By enabling you to place a particular collection of recipients in its own group. Once the group is set up, you just send your message to that group, and each member of the group gets a copy. What could be simpler?

To create a new group, open Address Book and follow these steps:

1. **Choose some or all of the contacts you want to include in your new group.** Hold down ⌘ and click each contact.

2. **Choose File ➪ New Group From Selection.** Address Book adds a new group and places the group name in a text box so you can edit it.

3. **Type a name for the new group, and then press Return.**

4. **To add another contact to the new group, click All group, click and drag the contact, and then drop it on the new group.**

A really useful variation on the group theme is the *Smart Group*. This is a group where each member has something in common. For example, consider the following scenarios:

- If everyone is employed by the same company, then the Company field is the same for each contact.

- If everyone works in the same department, then the Department field is identical for each contact.

- If everyone lives in the same city, then the City field for each contact is the same.

In other words, there's a specific field in each contact's card that contains the same data. When creating a Smart Group you specify not only the field on which to base the group, but also the value of the field that each contact must have in common. For example, if you want to create a group that consists of all your contacts who live in Schenectady, you need to set up the group so that it includes only those cards where the City field equals Schenectady.

So why is such a group smart? Because Address Book monitors your contacts. For example, consider a Smart Group of contacts in Schenectady:

- If Address Book sees that you've added a new card where the City field equals Schenectady, it automatically adds that contact to your Smart Group.

- If you edit an existing contact and change its City field to Schenectady, Address Book dutifully adds the edited contact to the Smart Group.

- If you delete a card that had Schenectady in the City field, Address Book removes the card from the Smart Group.

Now *that* is smart! Follow these steps to create a Smart Group:

1. **Choose File ⇨ New Smart Group.** You can also press Option+⌘+N. Address Book displays a dialog so you can define your Smart Group.

2. **Use the Smart Group Name text box to type a name for the new group.**

3. **Use the drop-down list on the left to choose the field you want to use as the basis for your Smart Group.**

4. **Use the middle drop-down list to select an operator.** The operators you see depend on the field type.

5. **Use the right text box to type the value you want contacts to match to qualify for membership in the group.** Figure 4.4 shows a filled-in dialog that defines a Smart Group.

6. **If you want to define multiple criteria, click + and repeat Steps 3 to 5.** Repeat as needed.

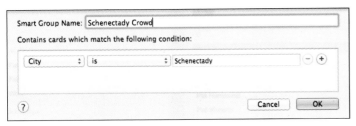

4.4 Use this dialog to define your Smart Group.

7. **If you added two or more criteria, use the Contains cards, which match the list to choose one of the following values:**

   - **all.** Choose this if you want Address Book to include in your Smart Group only those contacts that match every one of the criteria you added.

   - **any.** Choose this if you want Address Book to include in your Smart Group only those contacts that match at least one of the criteria you added.

8. **Click OK.** Address Book adds the Smart Group to the Group column.

With your regular group or Smart Group defined, you can now blast out email messages to the group in a couple of ways:

- **In Mail.** Start a new message and then either type the group name in the To text box, or click Address, and click and drag the group name in the Addresses window to the To field in the message.

- **In Address Book.** Click the group you want to use, right-click the group, and then click Send Email to *Group*, where *Group* is the name of the group.

**Note** If you don't see your most recently added group in the Addresses window, shut down and then restart Mail.

# Keeping track of birthdays

Do you have trouble remembering birthdays? If so, then I feel your pain because I, too, used to be pathetically bad at keeping birthdays straight in my head. And it's no wonder: These days you not only have to keep track of the birthdays of your family and friends, but more often than not, you also have to remember the birthdays of staff, colleagues, and clients as well. It's too much! My secret is that I simply gave up and outsourced the job to Address Book, which has a hidden Birthday field that you can use to store birthdates.

**Genius** Although the instructions in this section refer to birthdays, you can use similar techniques to help you keep track of any event. Remember that Address Book includes a Date field that lets you store data for any type of date.

To add the Birthday field to a card, choose the card and then choose Card⇨ Add Field⇨ Birthday. As you can see in Figure 4.5, Address Book adds the birthday field, and you then enter the month, day, and year. Click Edit when you're done.

4.5 Add the birthday field to those contacts whose birthdays you want to track.

**Genius** If you want to track the birthdays of a lot of people, don't add the birthday field by hand for each contact. Instead, add it to all contacts by customizing the card template to include the birthday field. Choose Card ⇨ Add Field ⇨ Edit Template. Use the Add Field list to choose birthday and then close the dialog.

## Creating a Smart Group that shows upcoming birthdays

If you start tracking birthdays in Address Book, you still have the problem of remembering when someone's birthday occurs. To avoid the embarrassment of sending belated birthday greetings, you can get Address Book to remind you when one or more birthdays are on the horizon.

You do this by setting up a Smart Group that contains only contacts who have upcoming birthdays; for example, within the next seven days. Here's how it's done:

1. **Choose File ⇨ New Smart Group.** You can also press Option+⌘+N. Address Book displays a dialog so you can define your Smart Group.

2. **Use the Smart Group Name text box to type a name for the new group.** For example, you could name the group Upcoming Birthdays.

3. **Use the drop-down list on the left to choose the birthday field.**

4. **Use the middle drop-down list to select the *is in the next* operator.**

5. **Use the text box next to the middle drop-down list to specify the number of days within which you want the birthdays to fall in order for a contact to be added to this Smart Group.**

6. **Make sure that you choose days from the drop-down list on the right.** Figure 4.6 shows a filled-in dialog for a Smart Group that looks for contacts who have birthdays within the next seven days.

7. **Click OK.** Address Book adds the Smart Group to the Group column.

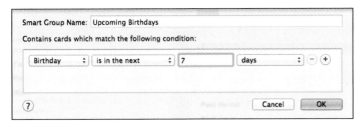

4.6 This Smart Group will show contacts who have birthdays within the next week.

The key here is that when Address Book detects a contact whose birthday falls within the timeframe specified by the group, it adds the contact to the group. Click the Smart Group to see which contact has an upcoming birthday, as shown in Figure 4.7.

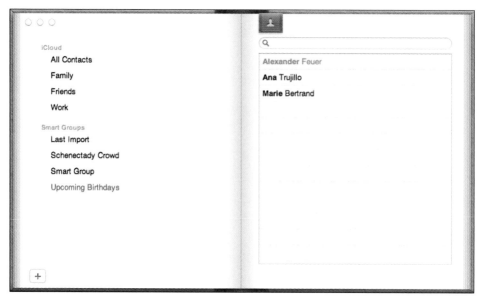

4.7 When the Smart Group detects a contact with an upcoming birthday, it automatically adds the contact to the group.

## Sending yourself an email birthday reminder

Although you can create a birthday Smart Group, which is useful, you might prefer a more direct reminder. You can build an Automator workflow that looks for those contacts who have birthdays next week and then sends you an email message to remind you. Here are the steps to follow:

1. **Choose Finder ⇨ Applications ⇨ Automator.** The Automator application appears.

2. **Click Workflow and then click Choose.**

3. **In the Library branch, choose Contacts.**

4. **Double-click the Find People with Birthdays action to add it to the workflow pane.**

5. **In the Find people whose birthday is drop-down list, choose Next Week.**

6. **Double-click the Get Contact Information action to add it to the workflow pane.**

7. **Select the check boxes to specify which information you want to include in the email message.** At the very least you should include the contact's name and birthday. Figure 4.8 shows an example.

8. **In the Library branch, choose Mail.**

9. **Double-click the New Mail Message action to add it to the workflow pane.**

10. **Fill in the To field and the Subject field.** The results of the Get Contact Information action are automatically added to the Message field.

4.8 Use the Get Contact Information action to select the data you want to include in the message.

11. **Double-click the Send Outgoing Messages action to add it to the workflow pane.**
    This action tells Automator to automatically send the email message. Figure 4.9 shows the workflow with the New Mail Message and Send Outgoing Messages actions added.

4.9 The New Mail Message and Send Outgoing Messages actions create and send the birthday reminder message.

12. **Save the workflow by choosing File ⇨ Save.**

**Genius**

If you're like me, you won't remember to run the birthday workflow. That's okay; MacBook Air can do it for you. In Automator, choose File ⇨ Save As, choose Application in the File Format drop-down list, and click Save. Open System Preferences, click Accounts, click your account, and click Login Items. Click + to open a Finder window, choose your birthday reminder application, and click Add. Every time you log in to MacBook Air, it automatically looks for contacts with birthdays on that day and sends them your greetings.

Be sure to run the workflow at the end of each week so you know whether you need to remember any upcoming birthdays. To run a workflow, open Automator, choose File ⇨ Open to open the workflow file, and then click Run.

## Automatically Send Birthday Greetings

When someone you know has a birthday, you can send a quick email to wish him a happy birthday. (I'm excluding family and good friends whom, of course, you'll call.) While sending an email is no big deal, MacBook Air gives you a way to automate this task, so let's check it out, just for fun:

1. **Choose Finder ⇨ Applications ⇨ Automator.** The Automator application appears.

2. **Click Workflow and then click Choose.**

3. **In the Library branch, choose Contacts.**

4. **Double-click the Find People with Birthdays action to add it to the workflow pane.**

5. **In the Find people whose birthday is drop-down list, choose Today.**

6. **In the Library branch, choose Mail.**

7. **Double-click the Send Birthday Greetings action to add it to the workflow pane.** This action enables you to specify a message and an image to include with the message.

8. **Type a birthday message and click the image you want to use.** You can also vary the images by selecting the Random Image for Each Recipient check box.

9. **Save the workflow.** Be sure to run the workflow each day.

# Importing contacts from Microsoft Outlook

If you've recently made the switch to Mac from Windows, you may have left behind a large collection of contact data in Microsoft Outlook. Don't worry; you don't have to manually type all that data into Address Book. Instead, you can export the data from Outlook and then import it into Address Book.

First, follow these steps to export your Outlook data:

1. **In Outlook, choose File ⇨ Options.** The Outlook Options dialog appears.

2. **Click Advanced.**

3. **Click Export.** The Import and Export Wizard appears.

4. **Choose Export to a file, and then click Next.**

5. **Choose Comma Separated Values (Windows), and then click Next.**

6. **Make sure the Contacts folder is selected, and then click Next.**

7. **Select a name and location for the file, and then click Next.** Ideally, save the file to a network location that you can access with MacBook Air. If MacBook Air and your Windows machine aren't on the same network, save the file anywhere you want and then send it to your MacBook Air email account as an attachment.

8. **Click Finish.** Outlook exports the contact data to a text file.

Now you can import the contacts into Address Book:

1. **In Address Book, choose File ⇨ Import.** The file selection dialog apears.

2. **Choose the text file that you exported earlier from Outlook, and then click Open.** Address Book displays the list of fields in the CSV file and how each field will map to an Address Book field, as shown in Figure 4.10.

4.10 Address Book maps each field in the exported file to a local field.

3. **Check to make sure the Address Book fields correspond with the correct fields in the text file.** In particular, if you see Do Not Import in the Address Book column, be sure to select a mapping for that field or Address Book will not import that data.

**Genius**
For some reason, Address Book doesn't do a good job of importing postal codes. That is, in the Text File Import dialog, it shows the Postal Code field as Empty, and although it recognizes the Home Postal Code fields from the Windows Address Book, it sets it to Do Not Import. To fix this, click Postal Code and then click Home Postal Code. For the business address, click Postal Code and then click Business Postal Code.

4. **Click OK.** Address Book imports the contact data.

**Note**
If nothing happens when you click OK, the exported text file likely contains one or more corrupted entries. Open the file in a text editor and look for lines that don't begin or end with a quotation mark, or for contact data that appears on two or more lines.

## Merging duplicate contacts into a single card

Despite your best organizational efforts, you might end up with duplicate contacts in your Address Book. This is particularly prone to happen when you import contacts from another program. Not to worry, though — Address Book has a handy feature that not only seeks out duplicate contacts, but also enables you to merge them into a single card.

In Address Book, choose Card⇨Look for Duplicates. Address Book examines the cards to see if it can find two with the same name. If it finds two such cards, it displays the dialog shown in Figure 4.11. Click Merge, and Address Book combines the data from both cards.

4.11 You see this dialog if Address Book finds duplicate contacts.

## Printing an envelope for a contact

You're probably so used to emailing and instant-messaging people these days that it comes as something of a shock when you find you have to — gasp! — send something by postal mail. If you're just dashing off an informal note, a handwritten envelope will do the trick. However, for more formal correspondence, you should send the envelope through your printer to make the address look more official.

Happily, Address Book knows how to deal with envelopes, and it offers all kinds of envelope-related bells and whistles to give you complete control over the look and configuration of both the recipient's address and your return address.

Follow these steps to print an envelope for an Address Book contact:

1. **Navigate to the contact for whom you want to create the envelope.**

2. **Choose File ⇨ Print.** You can also press ⌘+P. The Print dialog appears.

3. **Choose the printer you want to use from the Printer list.**

4. **Click Show Details to expand the Print dialog.**

5. **From the Style list, choose Envelopes, as shown in Figure 4.12.**

6. **Use the controls in the Label tab to configure the return address and contact address labels.**

7. **In the Layout tab, use the Layout list to select the type of envelope you're using.**

8. **Insert the envelope into your printer according to the printer's instructions.**

9. **Click Print.** Address Book prints the envelope.

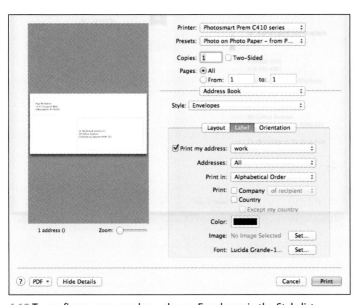

4.12 To configure your envelope, choose Envelopes in the Style list.

**Note**  If you're sending the envelope out of the country, you need to include the country in the recipient's address. To do this, select the Label tab's Country check box. If this is business correspondence, you should also select the Company check box, and choose the *for both* option in the list.

## Printing mailing labels for contacts

If you're working on your Christmas card list, a print newsletter, or a direct-mail marketing campaign, you eventually have to mail out a bunch of pieces. You can make this tedious chore quite a bit easier by printing a mailing label for each recipient. If you have all your recipients in your Address Book — ideally, they should be set up as a group —you can print those mailing labels right from the friendly confines of Address Book itself.

Follow these steps to print mailing labels for your Address Book contacts:

1. **Select the contacts for whom you want to create the mailing labels.**

2. **Choose File ⇨ Print.** You can also press ⌘+P. The Print dialog appears.

3. **Use the Printer list to choose the printer you want to use.**

4. **Click Show Details to expand the Print dialog.**

5. **In the Style list, choose Mailing Labels, as shown in Figure 4.13.**

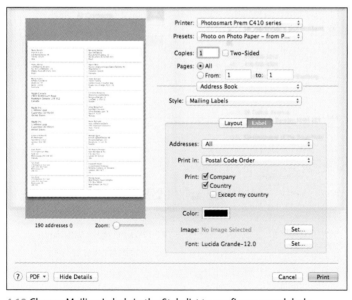

4.13 Choose Mailing Labels in the Style list to configure your labels.

6. **Use the controls in the Label tab to configure the contact address labels.**

7. **In the Layout tab, use the two Page lists to select the type of mailing labels you're using.**

8. **Insert the mailing labels into your printer according to the printer's instructions.**

9. **Click Print.** Address Book prints the mailing labels.

# Managing Your Appointments

When you meet someone and ask, "How are you?" the most common reply these days is a short one: "Busy!" We're all as busy as can be, and that places-to-go-people-to-see feeling is everywhere. All the more reason to keep your affairs in order, and that includes your appointments. MacBook Air comes with a program called iCal that you can use to create items called events, which represent your appointments. iCal acts as a kind of electronic personal assistant, leaving your brain free to concentrate on more important things.

## Setting up a meeting with a contact

If you want to add a meeting to iCal, you can set it up in the usual way by displaying the date, double-clicking the meeting time, and then typing a title for the new event. From there, you can double-click the event and specify the attendees.

**Note**  For the technique in this section to work, each contact you select must have at least one email address defined. Before proceeding, this is a good time to check that each contact you want to meet has an email address, and to include addresses for those contacts who don't.

However, if the meeting is with one or more people in your Address Book, there's an easier way you can add it to iCal:

1. **In iCal, make sure the day of the meeting is visible.**

2. **In Address Book, select the contact or contacts with whom you're having the meeting.**

3. **Click and drag the selected contacts and drop them inside iCal at the hour the meeting is to occur.** iCal creates a new event named Meeting with *Contact* (where *Contact* is the name of the first contact in your selection).

4. **Double-click the new event's time (the top half of the event).** As you can see in Figure 4.14, iCal automatically added each contact to the invitees list.

5. **Adjust the other event settings, as needed.**

6. **Click Send.** iCal sends a meeting invitation to each invitee.

# Adding an alert to an event

One of the truly useful secrets of stress-free productivity in the modern world is what I call the set-it-and-forget-it school of appointments. That is, you set up an appointment electronically and then get the same technology to remind you when the appointment occurs. That way, your mind doesn't have to waste energy fretting about missing the appointment because you know your technology has your back.

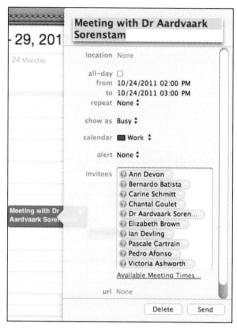

4.14 When you drag contacts from Address Book and drop them on a calendar, iCal sets up a meeting with the contacts as invitees.

With MacBook Air, the technology of choice for doing this is iCal's alert feature. When you add an alert to an event, iCal automatically displays a reminder of it. This reminder can be a message that pops up on the screen or an email sent to your address. You also get to choose when the alert triggers, such as a specified number of minutes, hours, or days before the event. You can even set up multiple alerts, just to be on the safe side.

**Note**

If you have a smartphone or other mobile device that can receive email, be sure to add the mobile device's email address to your Address Book card (use the Other email address field or create a custom field). This way, if you choose Email as the alert type, you can then choose your mobile device's address, which enables you to get the reminder while you're on the go.

Follow these steps to add an alert to an event:

1. **If you want to add the alert to a new event, display the date, click the time, and then choose File ⇨ New Event, or press ⌘+N.** Fill in the other event details as needed.

2. **Double-click the event, and then click Edit.**

3. **Click the alert list, and then click the type of alert you want:**

   - **Message.** Displays a pop-up message with the event particulars.

   - **Message with sound.** Displays a pop-up message accompanied by a sound effect that you choose.

   - **Email.** Sends a message with the event particulars to the email address specified in your Address Book card. If you have multiple addresses, you get to choose the one you prefer to use for the alert.

   - **Open file.** Opens a file or program that you specify.

   - **Run script.** Runs a script file that you specify.

4. **If the alert requires more data, such as choosing a sound file, email address, file, or script, use the list provided to make your choice.**

5. **Choose the reminder unit, such as minutes before or days before, and then set the number of units.** Figure 4.15 shows a completed example of an alert.

6. **Using the new alert list that appears below the alert you just created, follow Steps 3 to 5 to set up another alert for the same event, if needed.**

7. **Click Done.**

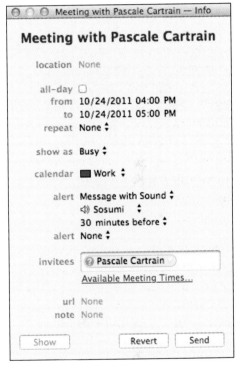

4.15 An event with a defined alert.

# Stopping automatic calendar additions

When you receive an email message that includes an invitation to an iCal event, your version of Mail might automatically add the event to your default calendar. (This was the default Mail behavior in recent versions, but not in the Lion version of Mail.) This is one of Mail's more annoying tendencies. I think most of us would rather add an invitation manually by clicking the link in the invite message, double-clicking the event in iCal, and then clicking either Accept or Decline.

Follow these steps to stop Mail from automatically adding event invitations to your calendar:

1. **In Mail, choose Mail ➪ Preferences.** The Mail preferences appear.
2. **Click the General tab.**
3. **In the Add invitations to iCal list, choose Never.**

# Setting up a custom repeat interval

One of iCal's truly great timesavers is the event repeat feature. It enables you to set up a single event and then get iCal to automatically repeat it at a regular interval. By default, you can repeat an event every day, week, month, or year. You can also continue the events indefinitely or end them after a specific number of times or on a specific date.

You can make this great feature even better by coming up with a custom repeat interval. For example, if you have an event that always occurs on the last Friday of every month, there's no way to schedule that using the regular repeat intervals. With a custom interval, however, it takes just a few mouse clicks.

Follow these general steps to set up a custom repeat interval:

1. **Create the event you want to repeat.** If you want to modify an existing event instead, double-click the event, and then click Edit.
2. **Click the repeat list, and then click Custom.**
3. **Use the Frequency list to select the base interval.** You have four choices:
   - **Daily.** Use the Every X day(s) text box to set the number of days you want to use for the interval.
   - **Weekly.** Use the Every X week(s) text box to set the number of weeks you want to use for the interval, and click the day of the week on which you want the events to fall.

- **Monthly.** Use the Every X month(s) text box to set the number of months you want to use for the interval. You can then either select the Each option and click the day of the month on which you want the events to fall, or select the On The option and choose a generic day on which you want the events to fall (such as the second Wednesday of the month).

- **Yearly.** Use the Every X year(s) text box to set the number of years you want to use for the interval, and then click the month in which you want the events to fall. You can also select the On The check box and then choose a generic day on which you want the events to fall (such as the last Friday of the year).

4. **Click OK.**

5. **Click Done.**

# Creating a calendar of birthdays

Earlier in this chapter, I covered how to add the birthday field to your Address Book cards to keep track of this special day for your friends, family, and even colleagues. However, you may find that you spend more time in iCal than in Address Book, so it would be nice to also add those birthdays to your calendar. You might groan at the thought of setting up a bunch of repeating all-day events, but you don't have to! With just a few mouse clicks, you can get iCal to do the heavy lifting for you. Here's how:

1. **Choose iCal ⇨ Preferences.** The iCal preferences appear.

2. **Click the General tab.**

3. **Select the Show Birthdays calendar check box, as shown in Figure 4.16.**

iCal sets up a Subscriptions section in the Calendars list and adds a calendar named Birthdays, as shown in Figure 4.17.

# Importing a calendar from Microsoft Outlook

If you're a reformed Microsoft Outlook user who has switched to iCal to manage your schedule, you may not relish the idea of

4.16 Select the Show Birthdays calendar check box to see Address Book birthdays in iCal.

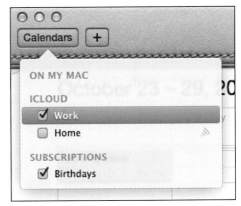

4.17 The Address Book birthdays appear in the Birthdays calendar.

89

adding all your pending appointments and events to iCal by hand. Fortunately, if you still have access to your Outlook data, you can export Outlook's Calendar data and then import it into iCal.

To start off, you need to export your Outlook Calendar data:

1. **In Outlook, choose the Calendar folder.**

2. **Tell Outlook that you want to send your calendar via email:**

   - **Outlook 2010.** In the Home tab, click Email Calendar. The Send a Calendar via Email dialog appears, as shown in Figure 4.18.

   - **Outlook 2007.** In the Navigation pane, click the Send a Calendar via Email link. The Send a Calendar via Email dialog appears.

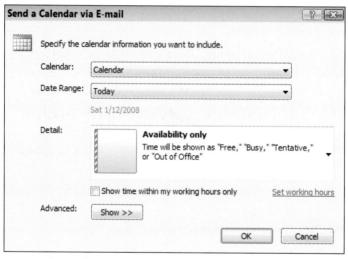

4.18 Use the Send a Calendar via Email dialog to export your Outlook calendar.

3. **If you have more than one calendar, use the Calendar drop-down list to choose the one you want to export.**

4. **Use the Date Range drop-down list to choose Whole calendar.**

5. **In the Detail list, choose Full details.**

6. **Click Show to expand the dialog.**

7. **If you have any private items in the calendar, select the Include details of items marked private check box to export those items.**

8. **In the Email Layout list, choose List of events.** The email layout isn't important, but choosing the List of events value is much better than choosing the Daily schedule value. This greatly reduces the amount of time Outlook spends composing the email message.

**Genius**

If you have had a large number of appointments in the past, exporting the whole calendar can take quite a while. To speed things up, use the Date Range drop-down list to choose Specify dates, and then specify the dates you want using the Start and End calendar controls.

9. **Click OK.** Outlook asks you to confirm that you want to send the whole calendar.

10. **Click Yes.** Outlook gathers the calendar data, starts a new email message, and attaches an iCalendar file that includes the data.

11. **You have two ways to proceed from here.**

   - **If your Windows PC and MacBook Air are on the same network, right-click the attached iCalendar file and click Copy.** Open a shared network folder that you can access with MacBook Air, and then press Control+V to paste the file into that folder.

   - **Use the To text box to type your iCloud address (or whatever email address you use with MacBook Air), and then click Send.** When you receive the iCalendar file, open the message, click and drag the attachment icon, and then drop the file on your desktop or in some other folder.

12. **Click Finish.** Outlook exports the contact data to a text file.

With that out of the way, you can now import the calendar into iCal:

1. **In iCal, choose File ➪ Import ➪ Import**. iCal displays the iCal: Import dialog.

2. **Navigate to the folder containing the iCalendar file, click it, and then click Import.** The Add events dialog appears.

3. **Choose the iCal calendar you want to use to import the Outlook events.** You can also choose New Calendar to import the events into a separate calendar.

4. **Click OK.** iCal imports the calendar data.

**Caution**

What happens if you have existing appointments that are the same as those you're importing? In that case, iCal overwrites the existing appointments.

# Sharing an iCloud calendar

There may be times when you want people to know what you're up to. For example, knowing when you have appointments scheduled helps other folks schedule their own appointments or events. If you have an iCloud account, you can use it to share your calendar with others, which enables your friends to keep tabs on you via iCal by either viewing your calendar online using a web browser, or by subscribing to your calendar (see the next section for the specifics).

Follow these steps to share an iCloud calendar:

1. **In iCal, click Calendars and then click the iCloud calendar you want to share.**

2. **Choose Calendar⇨Share Calendar.** The Share Calendar dialog appears.

3. **Use the Share calendar as text box to type the name under which you want your calendar shared.**

4. **Select the Only the people you invite option, as shown in Figure 4.19, to expand the dialog.** If you prefer to share your calendar with the whole world, select Everyone instead, and skip to Step 8.

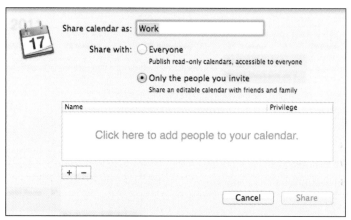

4.19 Use this expanded version of the Share Calendar dialog to choose who can view your shared calendar.

5. **Click +, begin typing a name, and then choose the invitees from the list that appears.**

6. **In the Privilege list, choose either Read & Write (to allow the person to edit your schedule) or Read Only.**

7. **Repeat Steps 5 and 6 to specify all your invitees.**

8. **Click Share.** iCal publishes the calendar to iCloud.

# Subscribing to a shared calendar

If you know someone who has published a calendar, you might want to keep track of that calendar within your version of iCal. You can do that by subscribing to the shared calendar. iCal sets up the shared calendar as a separate item in the Calendars section, so you can easily switch between your own calendar and the shared calendar.

Follow these steps to subscribe to a shared calendar:

1. **Specify the shared calendar address:**

   - **If you received an invitation via email, click the webcal link that appears in the body of the message.**

   - **If you need to type the address, start iCal, choose Calendar⇨Subscribe, and then use the Calendar URL text box to type the address of the shared calendar.** Figure 4.20 shows an example.

   4.20 Click the invitation link or type the address of a shared calendar to subscribe to it.

2. **Click Subscribe.** iCal locates the shared calendar and begins downloading the data. The "Calendar" Info dialog appears, as shown in Figure 4.21.

3. **If desired, type a new name for the calendar and choose a calendar color.**

4. **Deselect the check boxes beside the calendar items you want to keep: Alarms, Attachments, or Reminders.**

   4.21 Use the "Calendar" Info dialog to configure your calendar subscription.

5. **Choose a refresh interval from the Auto-refresh list if you want iCal to automatically refresh the calendar.** The options are Every 5 minutes, Every 15 minutes, Every hour, Every day, Every week, or No. Select No if you don't want iCal to automatically refresh.

6. **Click OK.** iCal creates a Subscriptions section and adds the calendar to that section.

**Genius**

To refresh the calendar manually, right-click the calendar and then click Refresh.

# How Do I Use MacBook Air to Organize My Online Life?

When you go online, you take your life along with you. Your online world becomes a natural extension of your real world. However, just because it's online doesn't mean the digital version of your life is any less busy, chaotic, or complex than the rest of your life. You can get the most out of your online presence with a few useful techniques for iCloud — MacBook Air's main online life tool.

# Getting More Out of iCloud

These days, the primary source of online chaos and confusion is the proliferation of services and sites that demand your time and attention. What started with web-based email has grown to a website, a blog, a photo-sharing site, online bookmarks, and perhaps a few social-networking sites, just to consume those last few precious moments of leisure time. You might be sitting in a chair, but you're being run ragged anyway!

A great way to simplify your online life is to get a free iCloud account. You get a one-stop web shop that includes email, an address book, a calendar, Find My iPhone (which locates not only lost iPhones, but also iPads and even your MacBook Air), and online storage for iWork documents. With Back to My Mac, you can log in to a home or office desktop remotely and download files from it, and even take control of the remote computer as if you were right there. With push technology, iCloud is able to automatically update all your computers for email, schedule changes, and the like.

After your account is up and running, you get to the iCloud login screen by going to www.icloud.com. Type your iCloud member name and password, and then click Sign In.

**Note**    If you don't want to commit any bucks before taking the iCloud plunge, you can sign up for a 60-day trial that's free and offers most of the features of a regular account. Go to www.me.com/ and click the sign up for a free trial link.

## Forwarding iCloud messages to another account

If you have a bunch of email addresses, chances are you have them all set up in MacBook Air's Mail application or some other email program because it's convenient to have all your messages in one spot. However, when you set up an iCloud account, your life become a tad less convenient because your iCloud messages reside only online, so now you have messages in two places: MacBook Air and iCloud. To fix this, you can forward your iCloud messages automatically to one of your existing accounts. That way, the messages come to your email program via that account, and you can once again work with all your messages from a single location.

Follow these steps to forward your iCloud messages to another email address:

1. **On any iCloud page, click the Switch Apps icon (the cloud) and then click Mail.** The iCloud Mail page appears.

2. **Click Actions (the gear icon) and then click Preferences.** The Preferences window appears.

3. **Click the General tab.**

4. **Select the Forward my email to check box.**

5. **Use the Forward my email to text box to type the address where you want the iCloud messages forwarded.** See Figure 5.1 for an example.

**5.1** You can configure your iCloud account to forward messages to another email address.

6. **If you don't want to save a copy of each message in your iCloud inbox, select the Delete messages after forwarding check box.**

7. **Click Done.**

## Configuring iCloud Mail not to show images in messages

In Chapter 6, you learn about the concept of the web bug and how images in HTML-formatted email messages can cause you to get more spam. Unfortunately, iCloud Mail is set up by default to automatically display images in all incoming messages, which is just plain dangerous. To fix this gaping privacy hole, you should configure iCloud Mail to not show images in messages. iCloud Mail is smart enough to recognize messages from people in your address book, so it will still show their images, but images from strangers (including spammers) will be blocked and can only be displayed manually.

Follow these steps to configure iCloud Mail not to not show remote images in HTML text messages:

1. **On any iCloud page, click the Switch Apps icon (the cloud) and then click Mail.** The iCloud Mail page appears.

2. **Click Actions (the gear icon) and then click Preferences.** The Preferences window appears.

3. **Click the General tab.**

4. **Deselect the Load images in HTML messages check box.**

5. **Click Done.**

If you get a message that contains remote images and the sender isn't in your iCloud Contacts list, you see the header shown in Figure 5.2. Click Load images to see the remote pictures.

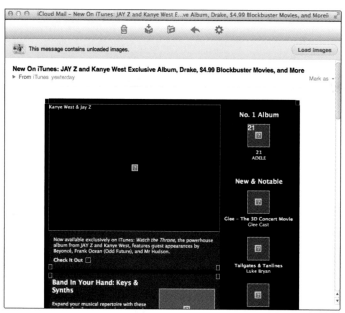

5.2 iCloud Mail now blocks images in messages from unknown senders; click Load images to see the images.

# Storing iWork documents online

Most of the info stored on your iCloud account — email messages, contacts, and appointments — is readily available online even if you're not using MacBook Air. For example, if you're at work, at a friend's house, or at an Internet café, you can still access your iCloud stuff by logging in to your account using whatever web browser is handy.

The same can't be said for important files on MacBook Air, because once you leave MacBook Air behind, you leave your files behind as well. Fortunately, iCloud can help here, too. Each iCloud account can store documents created using the iWork apps: Pages, Numbers, and Keynote. For example, if you use iWork on your MacBook Air, you can upload documents to iCloud. Also, if you use the iOS versions of any of these apps, you can set up automatic document synchronization between your iOS device and iCloud — and you can download any synced documents to your MacBook Air.

First, let's look at the steps required to upload an iWork document from MacBook Air to iCloud:

1. **On any iCloud page, click the Switch Apps icon (the cloud) and then click iWork.** The iCloud iWork page appears.

2. **Click the tab for the type of iWork document you want to upload: Keynote, Pages, or Numbers.**

3. **Click Actions (the gear icon), and then click Upload Document.** Your MacBook Air presents a file selection dialog.

4. **Click the document you want to upload, and then click Choose.** iCloud uploads the document and displays a thumbnail version. Figure 5.3 shows the Pages tab with a few documents uploaded.

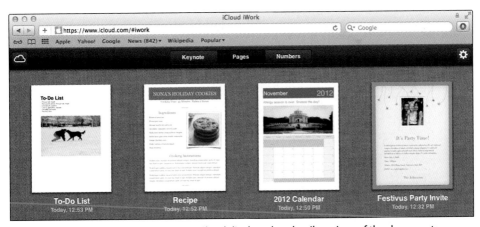

5.3 When you upload iWork documents, iCloud displays thumbnail versions of the documents.

If you also use any of the iWork apps on an iOS device, you can configure your device to sync iWork documents with your iCloud account. When you do this, two things happen:

● Any iWork documents you create on your iOS device appear automatically as thumbnails in the appropriate tab in the iCloud iWork page. Also, if you edit the document name or make changes to the first page of the document, those changes appear automatically in the iCloud thumbnails.

● If you upload an iWork document from your MacBook Air to iCloud, that document gets synced automatically to your iOS device.

Here are the steps to follow on your iOS device to configure iCloud document syncing:

1. **Set up your iCloud account on your iOS device, if you haven't done so already.**

2. **Tap Settings.** The Settings app appears.

3. **Tap iCloud.**

4. **Tap Documents & Data.**

5. **Tap the Documents & Data switch to On.**

6. **Return to the main Settings screen, scroll down to the Apps section, and tap the iWork app you want to sync.**

7. **Tap the Use iCloud switch to On.**

8. **Repeat Steps 6 and 7 for any other iWork apps you want to sync.**

When you open an iWork app on your iOS device, it begins syncing with your iCloud account. Figure 5.4 shows the Documents screen of the Pages app with the same thumbnails shown earlier in Figure 5.3.

If you create a new document on your iOS device, it gets synced to iCloud within a few seconds. If you later decide you want to work with that document on your MacBook Air, follow these steps to download it:

1. **On any iCloud page, click the Switch Apps icon (the cloud) and then click iWork.** The iCloud iWork page appears.

2. **Click the tab for the type of iWork document you want to download: Keynote, Pages, or Numbers.**

3. **Click the thumbnail of the document you want to download.**

4. **Click Download.** iCloud displays a list of compatible formats, as shown in Figure 5.5.

5. **Click the format you want to use for the downloaded document.** iCloud creates the document, downloads it, and then displays it in the appropriate application.

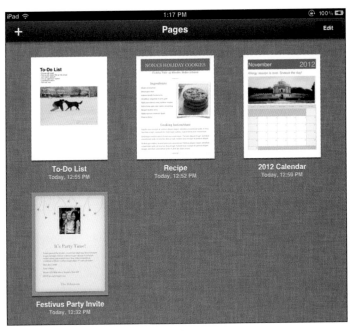

5.4 The iOS app syncs with your iCloud account.

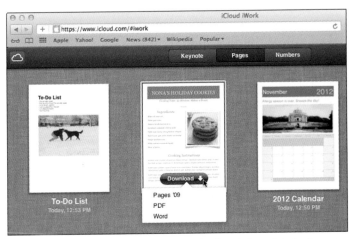

5.5 Click the document you want to download, and then click the format you want to use.

# Accessing MacBook Air over the Internet

Having a few important documents stored in iCloud can bail you out of a jam if you forget one of those files when you leave the house or office. Of course, a variation on Murphy's Law states that whatever file you need when you're away from MacBook Air will be a file that you didn't upload to iCloud.

Besides missing a particular file, another problem you may run into when you're on the road is missing a particular application. For example, suppose you have Microsoft Word on your home or office iMac but not on your MacBook Air. If you need to create a Word document or check a Word setting while you're using MacBook Air away from your home or office, you're out of luck.

You can solve both types of problems by accessing MacBook Air from a remote location using iCloud's Back to My Mac application. For this to work, you need to set up your two Macs as follows:

- **A local Mac that's running Lion (OS X 10.7) or later with a broadband connection to the Internet and signed in to an iCloud account that's a full member.**
- **A remote Mac that's running Lion (OS X 10.7) or later with a broadband connection to the Internet and signed in to the same iCloud account as the local Mac.** In the rest of this section, I assume that this remote Mac is your MacBook Air.

**Note**  Your local Mac also needs to connect to the network using a router that supports Universal Plug and Play (UPnP). Most modern routers support UPnP, so this shouldn't be a problem, but check your router manual to see how to ensure that UPnP is enabled.

If you have two such Macs, you're good to go. You can use the iCloud Back to My Mac feature, which enables you to use the remote Mac to connect to the local Mac via the iCloud account that they have in common. To configure Back to My Mac, you need to follow these steps on both Macs:

1. **Pull down the Apple menu and choose System Preferences.** The System Preferences window appears.
2. **Click iCloud.**
3. **Select the Back to My Mac check box, as shown in Figure 5. 6.**

The rest of the steps you only need to perform on the local Mac:

1. **Click Open Sharing Preferences.** The Sharing dialog appears.

2. **Select the Screen Sharing check box.** Screen sharing enables you to control the local Mac as though you were sitting in front of it.

3. **Select the Only these users option, click the Add button (+), click your username, and then click Select.** The username appears in the list, as shown in Figure 5.7.

4. **Select the File Sharing check box.** File Sharing gives you remote access to the local Mac's drives and folders.

5.6 In your iCloud account, select the Back to My Mac check box.

**Note**

Make sure MacBook Air (the Mac you'll be using for remote access) has a user account set up with the same name as the account you picked in Step 3.

You're now ready to make the remote connection. In the Finder sidebar of MacBook Air (the remote Mac), you see an icon for the local Mac under the Shared section. Click that icon to connect to the local Mac via the shared iCloud account. Figure 5.8 shows a File Sharing connection. If you want to switch to a Screen Sharing connection, click the Share Screen button.

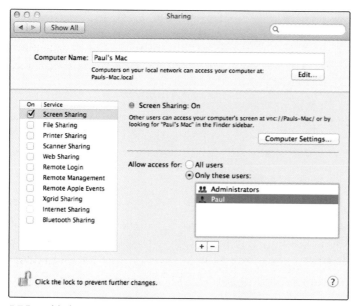

5.7 For added security, select Only these users, and then add your MacBook Air user account.

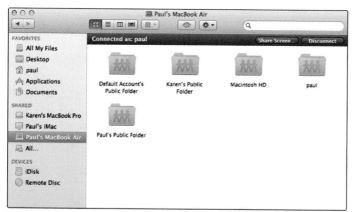

5.8 An icon for the local Mac appears in the Shared section of the sidebar on the remote Mac. Click the icon — Paul's MacBook Air, in this example — to make the connection via iCloud.

# Locating and Protecting a Lost MacBook Air

Depending on how you use your MacBook Air, you can easily end up with a pretty large chunk of your life residing on your machine. That sounds like a good thing, I know, but if you happen to lose your MacBook Air, you've also lost that chunk of your life, plus you've opened up a gaping privacy hole because anyone can now delve into your data.

If you've been backing up your MacBook Air regularly, then you can probably recover most or even all of that data. However, I'm sure you'd probably rather find your MacBook Air because it's expensive and there's just something creepy about the thought of some stranger rummaging through your stuff.

The old way of finding your MacBook Air consisted of scouring every nook and cranny that you visited before losing the machine and calling up various lost-and-found departments to see if anyone's turned it in. The new way to find your MacBook Air is a great new iCloud feature called Find My Mac. (You can also use this feature through Find My iPhone, an iOS app that you can download to your iPhone, iPad, or iPod touch through the App Store.) Find My Mac uses nearby wireless access points to locate the computer.

You can also use Find My Mac to send a message to the MacBook Air, remotely lock your MacBook Air, and, in a pinch, remotely delete your data. The next few sections provide the details.

**Genius**

To ensure that a thief can't mess with your MacBook Air, configure Mac OS X to require a password when it wakes from sleep mode. Open System Preferences, click Security & Privacy, and then click the General tab. Select the Require password check box, and choose Immediately in the pop-up. You should also select the Disable automatic login check box, as well as the Log out after check box. For the latter, use the associated pop-up to choose a relatively short timeout period, such as 5 minutes.

## Activating Find My Mac

Find My Mac works by using nearby wireless signals to triangulate the MacBook Air's current position. This triangulation is turned off by default, so you need to turn it on if you ever plan to use Find My Mac. Here are the steps to follow:

1. **Pull down the Apple menu and choose System Preferences.** The System Preferences window appears.

2. **Click iCloud.**

3. **Select the Find My Mac check box, as shown in Figure 5. 9.**

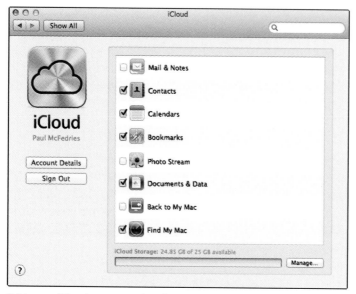

5.9 In your iCloud account, select the Find My Mac check box.

# Locating your MacBook Air on a map

With Find My Mac now active on your MacBook Air, you can use iCloud or the iOS app to locate it at any time. The next two sections show you the details.

## Locating your MacBook Air using iCloud

Follow these steps to see your lost MacBook Air on a map using iCloud:

1. **Sign in to your iCloud account.**

2. **Click the Switch Apps icon (the cloud) and then click Find My iPhone.** The iCloud Find My iPhone application appears.

3. **Click your MacBook Air in the My Devices list.** iCloud locates your MacBook Air on a map, as shown in Figure 5.10.

4. **To see if the location has changed, click the Refresh Location button (the circular arrow in the top-right corner of the My Devices list).**

**5.10** In the list of devices, tap your MacBook Air to locate it on a map.

## Locating your MacBook Air using the Find My iPhone app

Follow these steps to see your lost MacBook Air on a map using the Find My iPhone app on an iOS device:

1. **On an iOS device that has the Find My iPhone app installed, tap the app to launch it.** Find My iPhone prompts you to enter your Apple ID.

2. **Tap your Apple email address and password.** Note that you must use the same Apple ID as the one you used to activate the Find My iPhone setting on your MacBook Air.

3. **Tap Go.** The app signs in to your Apple account.

4. **If the app asks whether it can use your current location, tap OK.**

5. **If you're using Find My iPhone on an iPad, tap Devices.**

6. **In the list of devices, tap your lost MacBook Air.** The Find My iPhone app locates the MacBook Air on a map.

7. **To see if the location has changed, click the Refresh Location button (the circular arrow).** On the iPad version of the app, the Refresh Location button appears to the right of the Devices button; on the iPhone and iPod touch, it appears in the lower-left corner of the screen.

107

# Sending a message to your MacBook Air

If you think another person has your MacBook Air, you can try to contact the person by sending a message to the MacBook Air using the iCloud Find My iPhone application, or the iOS Find My Mac app. Here's how it works:

1.  **Tap or click your MacBook Air in the list of devices.** Find My iPhone locates your MacBook Air on a map.

2.  **Tap or click the blue More icon to the right of your MacBook Air name.** Find My iPhone displays information about your MacBook Air as well as buttons for various actions you can take.

3.  **Tap or click Display Message or Play Sound.** Find My iPhone displays the Display a Message dialog.

4.  **Type your message.** Figure 5.11 shows an example.

5.  **If you want to be sure the other person sees your message, leave the Play Sound switch in the On position.**

6.  **Tap or click Send.** Find My iPhone sends the message, which then appears on the MacBook Air screen, as shown in Figure 5.12.

5.11 You can send a message to your lost MacBook Air.

5.12 The message appears on the MacBook Air screen.

# Remotely locking the data on your MacBook Air

While you're waiting for the other person to return your MacBook Air, you probably don't want that person rummaging around in your stuff. To prevent that, you can remotely lock the MacBook Air. Here's how:

1.  **Tap or click your MacBook Air in the Devices list.** Find My iPhone locates your MacBook Air on a map.

2.  **Tap or click the blue More icon to the right of your MacBook Air name.** Find My iPhone displays information about your MacBook Air as well as buttons for various actions you can take.

3. **Tap or click Remote Lock.** Find My iPhone displays the Remote Lock dialog, as shown in Figure 5.13.

4. **Tap or click the numbers in the keypad to enter a four-digit passcode, and then click next.**

5. **Reenter a four-digit passcode.** Find My Mac remotely locks the MacBook Air.

# Remotely deleting the data on your MacBook Air

If you can't get the other person to return your MacBook Air and your MacBook Air contains sensitive or confidential data — or if it just

5.13 To prevent anyone from messing with your lost MacBook Air, you can apply a passcode lock remotely.

contains that big chunk of your life I mentioned earlier — you can use the Find My iPhone app or iCloud's Find My iPhone feature to take the drastic step of remotely wiping all the MacBook Air's data. Here's what you do:

1. **Tap or click your MacBook Air in the Devices list.** Find My iPhone locates your MacBook Air on a map.

2. **Tap or click the blue More icon to the right of your MacBook Air name.** Find My iPhone displays information about your MacBook Air as well as buttons for various actions you can take.

3. **Tap or click Remote Wipe.** Find My iPhone prompts you to enter a passcode.

4. **Tap or click the numbers in the keypad to enter a four-digit passcode, and then click next.**

5. **Reenter a four-digit passcode.** Find My iPhone displays the Remote Wipe dialog.

6. **Type a message that will appear on the MacBook Air screen after it has been wiped, as shown in Figure 5.14.**

5.14 If you're certain your lost MacBook Air is a lost cause, you can remotely erase all its data.

7. **Tap or click Wipe.** Find My iPhone remotely wipes all the data from the MacBook Air.

# Can MacBook Air Help Me Communicate More Effectively?

You might think MacBook Air is all about data — creating documents, processing photos, making movies, researching stuff on the Internet, and so on. Well, sure, MacBook Air can help you do all of that, and help you do it with style and aplomb. But you can make a strong case that MacBook Air is really all about communication. After all, you probably spend great chunks of time with MacBook Air sending email, reading and responding to incoming messages, and having video chats with your buddies. It's a veritable communications frenzy. But as you see in this chapter, MacBook Air can help you get more out of this part of your life.

# Improving Your Email Life

Email has been called the "killer app" of the Internet, and it certainly deserves that title. Yes, chat and instant messaging are popular. Social networks, such as Facebook, Twitter, and LinkedIn get lots of press, and microblogging sites, like Tumblr, appeal to a certain type of person. Not everyone uses these services, but it's safe to say that almost everyone uses email. In fact, if you're like the majority of the world, you probably use email all day long. This means that learning a few efficient email techniques can make your day a bit easier and save you time for more important pursuits.

## Configuring Mail not to show images in messages

Lots of messages nowadays come not just as plain text, but also with fonts, colors, images, and other flourishes. This fancy formatting, called either rich text or HTML, makes for a more pleasant email experience, particularly for images. Who doesn't like a bit of eye candy to brighten the day? Unfortunately, however, not all images are benign. A *web bug* is an image that resides on a remote server and is added to an HTML-formatted email message by referencing an address on the remote server. Images and other objects that reside on a remote server and are not embedded in the message are called *external content*. When you open the message, Mail uses the address to download the image for display within the message.

**Note** HTML stands for Hypertext Markup Language and is the method that folks use to put together most web pages. It was so named because it is similar in spirit to how an editor would "mark up" a manuscript, or show the printer how it is to be published.

That sounds harmless enough, but if the message is junk email, the image address likely also contains either your email address or a code that points to your email address. So when the remote server gets a request for the URL, it knows not only that you've opened the message, but also that your email address is legitimate. Not surprisingly, spammers use web bugs all the time because, for them, valid email addresses are a form of gold.

Unfortunately, the Mail application isn't entirely hip to the web bug menace. On the positive side, if it detects that a message is spam, it blocks remote images from that message, as shown in Figure 6.1. If the message is actually legitimate, you can click Load Images to see whatever pictures the message has to offer.

On the negative side, Mail shows remote images in any message that it doesn't think is spam. Mail's junk mail filtering feature works well, but it doesn't catch every single spam message that comes your way. This means that it could show remote images from any piece of junk mail that it misses.

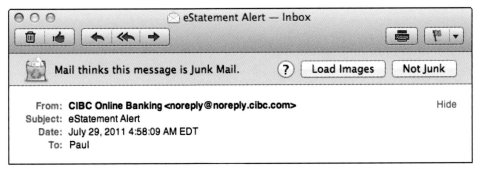

6.1 If Mail detects a junk message, it displays this header and prevents the message from loading any remote images.

To prevent that, you can configure Mail not to show remote images in any HTML or rich text message:

1. **Choose Mail ⇨ Preferences.** The Mail preferences appear.

2. **Click the Viewing icon.**

3. **Deselect the Display remote images in HTML messages check box, as shown in Figure 6.2.**

Now if you get a nonspam message that contains remote images, you see the header shown in Figure 6.3. Click Load Images to see the remote pictures.

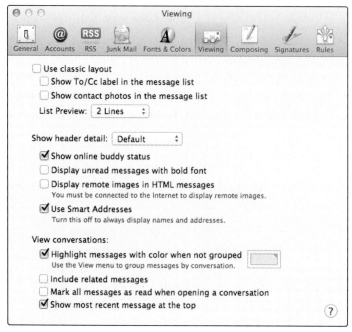

6.2 You can configure Mail not to show remote images in any HTML or rich text message.

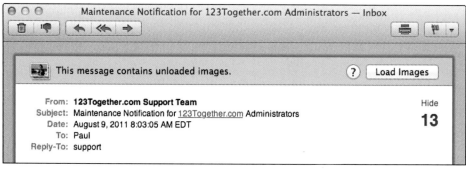

6.3 Mail now blocks remote images in nonjunk messages. Click Load Images to see them.

# Moving junk messages to the Junk folder

It's sad to say that there are no longer any spam-free zones. If you have an Internet-based email account, you get spam. End of story. In fact, you most likely don't get only one or two spams a day, but more like one or two dozen. Actually, one or two hundred (shudder) is no longer an unusually high amount. That's not surprising because spam now accounts for the majority of the billions of messages sent every day, and on some days it even accounts for 90 percent of all sent messages!

## Avoiding Spam

It is no longer possible to avoid spam, but there are some things you can do to minimize how much of it you have to wade through each day:

- **Never use your actual email address in a forum or newsgroup account.** The most common method that spammers use to gather addresses is to harvest them from online posts. One common tactic you can use is to alter your email address by adding text that invalidates the address, but is still obvious for other people to figure out. Here's an example: yourname@yourisp. remove-this-to-email-me.com.

- **When you sign up for something online, use a fake address if possible.** If you need or want to receive email from the company and must use your real address, make sure you deactivate any options that ask if you want to receive promotional offers. Alternatively, use an address from a free web-based account (such as a Yahoo! account), so that any spam you receive goes there instead of to your main address.

- **Never open suspected spam messages or display them in the preview pane.** Doing so can sometimes notify the spammer that you've opened the message, which confirms that your address is legitimate.

- **If you see a message in your Inbox that you're sure is spam, don't click it.** Clicking it displays the message in the preview pane. Instead, right-click the message and then choose Delete.

- **Never, I repeat, *never*, respond to spam.** Don't respond, even to an address within the spam that claims to be a "removal" address. By responding to the spam, you prove that your address is legitimate, so you just end up getting more spam.

If you still get spam despite taking precautions, Mail's Junk Mail feature is your next line of defense. It's a spam filter that examines each message you receive to look for telltale signs of spamminess (as anti-spam types call it). If Mail determines that a message is spam, it displays the message's details in a light-brown text. When you click the message, Mail displays the header, as shown previously in Figure 6.1.

This is all well and good, but it does mean that you end up with junk mail mixed in with your legitimate messages, which, given the explicit nature of so many spam subject lines these days, isn't a desirable state of affairs. It would be much better if Mail just shuffled all suspected spam to the Junk mailbox. Here's how to configure Mail to do just that:

1.  **If you have any spam in your Inbox that isn't marked as junk mail, right-click each message and then choose Mark ⇨ As Junk Mail.**

2.  **Choose Mail ⇨ Preferences.** The Mail preferences appear.

3.  **Click the Junk Mail icon.**

4.  **In the When junk mail arrives section, select the Move it to the Junk mailbox option (see Figure 6.4).** Mail asks if you want to move all the messages currently marked as junk to the Junk mailbox.

5.  **Click Move.**

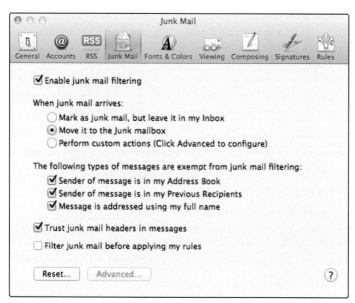

6.4 You can configure Mail to automatically move messages marked as junk to the Junk mailbox.

Be sure to check the Junk mailbox from time to time to make sure that Mail hasn't caught any *false positives*, that is, legitimate messages marked as junk. If you do see a legit message in the Junk mailbox, right-click the message, choose Mark⇨As Not Junk Mail, and then move the message back to the Inbox.

**Genius**

Checking the Junk mailbox is never fun because it means dealing directly with messages that are usually either offensive or annoying (or both). To make this distasteful chore less onerous, turn off the preview pane before displaying the Junk mailbox. To toggle the preview pane off and on, double-click the vertical bar that separates the folder content from the preview pane.

If you don't want to bother with the often unsavory chore of deleting junk mail, you can get Mail to handle it for you automatically. Choose Mail⇨Preferences, click the Accounts icon, click the account you want to work with, and then click the Mailbox Behaviors tab. In the Delete junk messages when list, select an interval after which spam is canned: One day old, One week old, One month old, or Quitting Mail.

## Leaving incoming messages on the server

In today's increasingly mobile world, it's not unusual to find that you need to check the same email account from multiple devices. For example, you might want to check your business account not only from your work computer, but also from your home computer, your MacBook Air while traveling, or from a smartphone or other mobile device while commuting.

If you need to check email on multiple devices, you can take advantage of how email messages are delivered over the Internet. When someone sends you a message, it doesn't come directly to your Mac. Instead, it goes to the server that your ISP (or your company) has set up to handle incoming messages. This is often called a POP (Post Office Protocol) server. When you ask Apple Mail to check for new messages, it communicates with the POP server to see if any messages are waiting in your account. If so, Mail downloads those messages to MacBook Air and then instructs the server to delete the copies of the messages stored on the server.

The trick, then, is to configure Mail so that it leaves a copy of the messages on the POP server after you download them. That way, the messages are still available when you check messages using another device. Fortunately, the intuitive folks who designed Mail must have understood this, because the program automatically sets up POP accounts to do just that. (A POP account is an account you have with an ISP — this doesn't apply to iCloud accounts.) Specifically, after you download any messages from the POP server to MacBook Air, Apple Mail waits a week before deleting the messages.

However, if you have multiple Macs, this setting doesn't work well because you want only one of the Macs to control when messages get deleted from the server. Here's a good strategy that ensures you can download messages on all your devices, but prevents messages from piling up on the server:

- Let your main Mac be the computer that controls deleting the messages from the server. You can either leave the setting at the default (to delete after one week), or you can adjust the timing, as described in the next set of steps.

- Set up all your other devices to leave a copy of each message on the server.

If you want to adjust either how long your main Mac waits before deleting messages from the server, or if you want to configure a Mac (say, MacBook Air) to leave messages on the server, follow these steps to configure this feature:

1. **Choose Mail ⇨ Preferences.** The Mail preferences appear.

2. **Click the Accounts icon.**

3. **In the Accounts list, click the icon for the POP account with which you want to work.**

4. **Click the Advanced tab.**

5. **Perform one of the following actions, depending on how you want MacBook Air to treat messages on the server:**

   - **Delete server messages after a while.** Leave the Remove copy from server after retrieving a message check box selected. Then use the list below it to choose the interval you want to use: After one day, After one week, or After one month.

   - **Leave copies of messages on the server.** Deselect the Remove copy from server after retrieving a message check box.

# Skipping large incoming messages

Most POP mail hosts set a limit on the size of the email messages they will handle. It might be as small as 1MB or as large as 20MB. Any message larger than the specified size won't go through.

**Genius**

Another good time to skip large messages is when you're using a slow Internet connection. For example, if you're accessing the Internet over a dial-up connection, you might want to skip messages larger than, say, 100K. When you have MacBook Air on a faster connection, be sure to remove this threshold so you don't miss anything important.

If your email server has such a restriction, here's a problem you've probably encountered a time or two: Mail tries to download your messages, but it gets stuck because one of your messages is too large for your server to handle. Mail can't get past the too-large message, so all your other messages get backed up behind it.

Solving this problem often requires a call to the mail host's tech support line (never a pleasant experience), but Mail offers a work-around. You can configure it not to download (or, more accurately, to ask you whether you want to download) messages larger than your POP mail server allows. Here's how it's done:

1. **Choose Mail ⇨ Preferences.** The Mail preferences appear.
2. **Click the Accounts icon.**
3. **In the Accounts list, click the icon for the POP account you want to work with.**
4. **Click the Advanced tab.**
5. **In the Prompt me to skip messages over text box, type the number of KB you want to use as a threshold.** For example, if your POP mail host restricts messages to 4MB, then you'd type 4000 in the text box, as shown in Figure 6.5.

If there's a downside to setting this option, it's that Mail gives you only a few seconds to make your decision. When Mail checks for new messages (or when you click the Get Mail button in the toolbar) and it finds a too-large message waiting on the server, you see the dialog shown in Figure 6.6. You have only 15 seconds to click one of the following buttons:

- **Skip.** Leaves the message on the server. Note that Mail (sensibly) doesn't try to download the message again until your next Mail session.
- **Delete.** Permanently deletes the message.
- **Download.** Downloads the message to Mail. This is the default action that Mail takes after the 15 seconds are up.

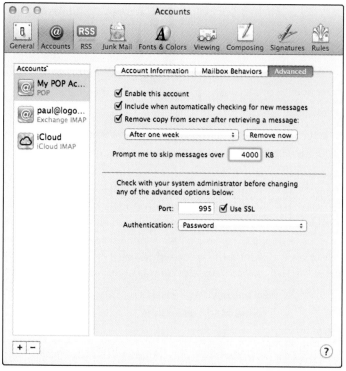

6.5 To avoid problems that overly large messages create, configure Mail so it prompts you before downloading messages larger than your POP mail server allows.

6.6 Mail displays this dialog when it detects an incoming message larger than the threshold you specified. Act fast!

## Sending email with a different server port

For security reasons, some Internet service providers (ISPs) insist that all of their customers' outgoing mail must be routed through the ISP's Simple Mail Transport Protocol (SMTP) server. This usually is not a big deal if you use an email account that the ISP maintains. However, it can lead to the following problems if you use an account provided by a third party (such as your website host):

- Your ISP might block messages sent using the third-party account because it thinks you're trying to relay the message through the ISP's server (a technique often used by spammers).

- You might incur extra charges if your ISP allows only a certain amount of SMTP bandwidth per month, or a certain number of sent messages, whereas the third-party account offers higher limits or no restrictions at all.

- You might have performance problems, such as the ISP's server taking much longer to route messages than the third-party host.

You might think that you can solve these problems by specifying the third-party host's SMTP server in the account settings. However, this doesn't usually work because outgoing email is sent by default through port 25. When you use this port, you must also use the ISP's SMTP server.

To work around this problem, many third-party hosts offer access to their SMTP server via a port other than the standard port 25. For example, the iCloud SMTP server (smtp.me.com) also accepts connections on port 587. Check your host's support pages or call your host to find out the nonstandard port it uses, if any.

**Note**

Many hotels and Wi-Fi hotspots block access to port 25.

Here's how to use Mail to configure an email account to use a nonstandard SMTP port:

1. **Choose Mail ⇨ Preferences.** The Mail preferences appear.

2. **Click the Accounts icon.**

3. **In the Accounts list, click the icon for the POP account with which you want to work.**

4. **Click the Account Information tab.**

5. **In the Outgoing Mail Server (SMTP) list, choose Edit Server List.**

6. **In the list of SMTP servers, click the server with which you want to work.**

7. **Click the Advanced tab.**

8. **Select the Use custom port option.**

9. **In the Use custom port text box, type the port number you want to use.** For example, Figure 6.7 shows an SMTP server configured to use port 2500.

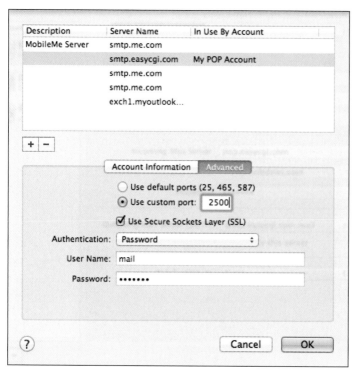

| Description | Server Name | In Use By Account |
|---|---|---|
| MobileMe Server | smtp.me.com | |
| | smtp.easycgi.com | My POP Account |
| | smtp.me.com | |
| | smtp.me.com | |
| | exch1.myoutlook... | |

+  −

| Account Information | Advanced |
|---|---|

○ Use default ports (25, 465, 587)
● Use custom port: [ 2500 ]
☑ Use Secure Sockets Layer (SSL)

Authentication: [ Password ⇕ ]
User Name: [ mail ]
Password: [ •••••• ]

(?)                    Cancel    OK

6.7 Select the Use custom port option. In the text box, specify the nonstandard port you want for the SMTP server.

## Sending all messages from the same account

If you have two or more email accounts set up, you may have noticed one of Mail's quirkier behaviors. When you compose a message, the account you see in the From list isn't always the same account. For example, if you have both an iCloud and a POP account set up, sometimes the From list shows the iCloud account. At other times, it shows the POP account. What's the story?

The background here is that Mail keeps track of the last mailbox you viewed, and it uses the account associated with that mailbox in the From list when you next go to compose a message. That actually makes a bit of sense when you think about it. For example, if you're currently working in a mailbox associated with your iCloud account and you start a new message, there's a good chance that you want to send that message using your iCloud account.

However, it's much more likely that you want to use a single account to send most of your messages, so Mail's default behavior is inefficient. Here's how to fix it:

1. **Choose Mail ⇨ Preferences.** The Mail preferences appear.

2. **Click the Composing icon.**

3. **Use the Send new messages from list to choose the account you want to set as the default sending account (see Figure 6.8).**

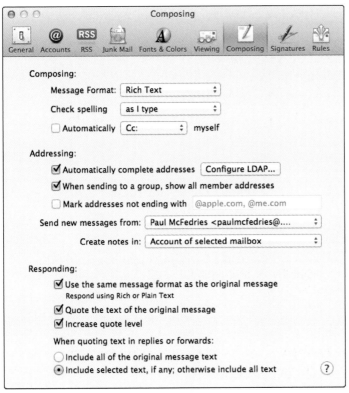

6.8 Use the Send new messages from list to choose the default account for sending messages.

## Setting up rules to process incoming messages

With email now fully entrenched in the business (and even home) landscape, email chores proba- bly take up more and more of your time. In addition to composing, reading, and responding to messages, basic maintenance — flagging, moving, deleting, and so on — also takes up large chunks of otherwise productive time.

To help ease the time crunch, Mail lets you set up rules that perform actions in response to specific events. Here are just a few of the things you can do with rules:

- Move an incoming message to a specific mailbox if the message contains a particular keyword in the subject or body, or if it's from a particular person.

- Automatically delete messages with a particular subject or from a particular person.

- Flag messages based on specific criteria (such as keywords in the subject line or body).

- Have Mail notify you when a high-priority message arrives, either by playing a sound or bouncing the Mail icon in the Dock.

For example, you may have noticed that any messages you get from Apple appear with a blue background. This is because Mail comes with a predefined rule that looks for messages from Apple and sets the background color of those messages to blue.

**Genius**

You can save yourself a bit of time by creating a rule based on an existing message. For example, you could create a rule that uses the sender's address or the message's Subject line. To do this, click the message you want to use before going through the steps to set up your own rule.

Here's how you set up your own rule:

1. **If you want Mail to apply your new rule to the messages in a particular mailbox, select that mailbox.**

2. **Choose Mail ⇨ Preferences.** The Mail preferences appear.

3. **Click the Rules icon.**

4. **Click Add Rule.**

5. **Use the Description text box to type a name for the rule.**

6. **Specify the conditions that an incoming message must satisfy to trigger the rule.** You use the list on the far left to select the message data that you want Mail to check, such as the message priority, the From address, the Subject line, or the message content. Whether you need to specify more information to complete the criterion depends on the data (see Figure 6.9 for examples).

   - **Some data doesn't require more information.** For example, if you choose Priority is High, the condition is met if an incoming message uses the High priority level.

   - **Some data requires that you specify one other bit of information.** For example, if you choose Account, you must also specify one of your email accounts. The condition is met if an incoming message is sent to that account.

- **Some data requires both an operator and some specific information.** For example, if you choose From, you must also specify an operator — such as Contains or Is Equal To — and then some text. The condition is met if an incoming message has From text that matches what you specify.

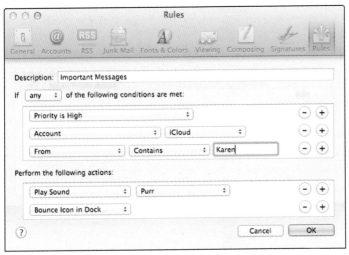

6.9 Some examples of the conditions you can specify for a rule.

7. **To add another condition, click the plus sign (+).**

8. **Repeat Steps 6 and 7 until you have specified all the conditions for your rule.**

9. **If you specified two or more conditions, use the If X of the following conditions are met list (where X is Any or All) to decide how Mail applies the conditions.**

   - **Any.** Choose this item to have Mail trigger the rule only if an incoming message meets at least one of the conditions.

   - **All.** Choose this item to have Mail trigger the rule only if an incoming message meets every one of the conditions.

10. **Use the controls in the Perform the following actions section to specify what you want Mail to do when an incoming message meets your conditions.** As with conditions, the action you choose may require you to specify more information (such as choosing a sound, as shown in Figure 6.9).

11. **To add another action, click the plus sign (+).**

12. **Repeat Steps 10 and 11 until you have specified all the actions for your rule.**

13. **Click OK.** Mail asks if you want to apply the new rule to the messages in the current mailbox.

14. **Click Apply if you want to run the rule now.** Otherwise, click Don't Apply.

# Creating a Smart Mailbox

A *Smart Mailbox* is one that consolidates all of your messages that meet one or more conditions. It doesn't matter which mailbox the messages currently reside in — it could be any Inbox, the Sent box, or even the Trash. Once you set up a Smart Mailbox, Mail copies the applicable messages to the Smart Folder, and if any incoming messages meet the criteria, they also are copied to the Smart Folder. (In both cases, the original messages remain in their current folders.) It's a great way to keep your messages organized without having to do any of the organizing yourself.

Follow these steps to set up your own Smart Mailbox:

1. **If you want to set up the Smart Mailbox based on the data in an existing message, click the message.**

2. **Choose Mailbox ⇨ New Smart Mailbox.**

3. **Use the Smart Mailbox Name text box to type a name for the Smart Mailbox, as shown in Figure 6.10.**

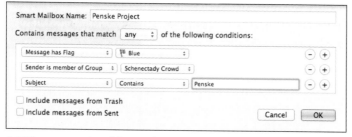

6.10 Some examples of the conditions you can specify for a Smart Mailbox.

4. **Specify a condition that messages must satisfy to be put in the Smart Mailbox.** You use the list on the far left to select the message data that you want Mail to use, such as the message priority, the From address, the Subject line, or the message content.

Whether you need to specify more information to complete the criterion depends on the data (see Figure 6.10 for examples).

- **Some data doesn't require more information.** For example, if you choose Message is Flagged, the condition is met if a message has a flag.

- **Some data requires you to specify one other bit of information.** For example, if you choose Sender is member of Group, you must also specify one of your Address Book groups. The condition is met if a message was sent from someone in that group.

- **Some data requires both an operator and some specific information.** For example, if you choose Subject, you must also specify an operator, such as Contains or Begins With, and then some text. The condition is met if a message has Subject text that matches what you specify.

5. **To add another condition, click the plus sign (+).**

6. **Repeat Steps 4 and 5 until you have specified all the conditions for your Smart Mailbox.**

7. **If you specified two or more conditions, use the Contains messages that match _X_ of the following conditions list (where _X_ is Any or All) to decide how Mail applies the conditions.**

   - **Any.** Choose this item to have Mail add a message to the Smart Mailbox if it meets at least one of the conditions.

   - **All.** Choose this item to have Mail add a message to the Smart Mailbox if it meets all of the conditions.

8. **If you want to include any Trash mailbox messages that satisfy the conditions, select the Include messages from Trash check box.**

9. **If you want to include any Sent mailbox messages that satisfy the conditions, select the Include messages from Sent check box.**

10. **Click OK.** Mail creates the Smart Mailbox and populates it with all of the messages that meet your conditions.

# Video Calling with FaceTime

One of the most welcome MacBook Air features is the built-in iSight camera, not only because you can use it to have all kinds of fun taking silly Photo Booth pictures, but also because it lets you take advantage of Apple's amazing FaceTime feature, which lets you make video calls where you can actually see the other person face to face. It's an awesome feature, but to use it the other person must be using an iPad 2 or later, an iPhone 4 or later, a 4th-generation iPod touch or later, or another Mac with a video camera and the FaceTime application installed. Note that for Mac OS X Lion (10.7), FaceTime is installed by default; for Mac OS X Snow Leopard (10.6.6), FaceTime is available through the App Store for 99 cents. You'll also need an Apple ID.

**Note**  In previous versions of FaceTime, both of you also needed to be on a Wi-Fi connection. That restriction has been dropped, and you can now conduct FaceTime calls with iPhone and iPad users who are on a 3G connection.

## Configuring FaceTime

The first time you launch FaceTime, you need to run through a one-time configuration procedure. Here's how it works:

1. **In the Dock, click FaceTime.** The FaceTime window appears.
2. **Type your Apple ID email address.**
3. **Type your Apple ID password.**
4. **Click Sign In.** FaceTime prompts you to specify an email address that people can use to contact you via FaceTime.
5. **If the address you prefer to use is different than your Apple ID, type the address you want to use.**
6. **Click Next.** FaceTime verifies your Apple ID and then displays a list of contacts.

## Initiating a FaceTime call

Once you sign in with your Apple ID, you can use the FaceTime application to connect with another person and conduct a video chat. How you connect with the other person depends on what device he or she is using for FaceTime. If the person is using a Mac, an iPad, or an iPod touch, you'd use whatever email address the person has designated as his or her FaceTime contact address, as described in the previous section. If the person is using an iPhone, you'd use that person's mobile number to make the connection.

To initiate a FaceTime call, use either of the following techniques:

- If the other person is in your Contacts list, click Contacts and then click the person you want to call. If the person has multiple contacts items (phone numbers and email addresses), click the item you want to use to place the call.

- If you've recently made a FaceTime call to someone, click the Recents icon and then click the FaceTime call.

If an iOS user or FaceTime for Mac user calls you, you see the message *"Name would like FaceTime"* (where *Name* is the caller's name if he or she is in your Contacts list), as shown in Figure 6.11. Click Accept and your video call connects, just like that. You see your caller's (hopefully) smiling face in the full iPhone screen, and your own mug in a picture-in-picture (PIP) window, as shown in Figure 6.12.

6.11 When a FaceTime user calls you, click Accept to initiate a FaceTime video call.

6.12 Face-to-face calling on the MacBook Air.

**Genius**

If you FaceTime call someone frequently, add that person to the FaceTime app's Favorites list. Click the Favorites icon, click +, click the contact, and then click the phone number or email address you want to use.

**Genius** Your PIP window appears by default in the upper-right corner. If you prefer a different position, click and drag the PIP window to any corner of the screen.

The FaceTime calling screen includes three buttons in the menu bar:

- **Mute.** Click this icon (it's the one on the left) to mute the sound from your end of the conversation (you can still hear sound from the other person's end).

**Note** You might prefer to conduct your video chat in landscape mode, which shows more to the left and right of the caller. Choose Video ⇨ Use Landscape, or press ⌘+R.

- **End.** Click this button (it's the one in the middle) to end the call.
- **Enter Full Screen.** Click this button (it's on the right) to switch to full-screen mode. You can also press Shift+⌘+F.

## Disabling FaceTime

There will certainly be times when you simply don't want a face-to-face conversation, no matter who's calling. Perhaps you're in a secret location or you just don't look your best that day. Whatever the reason, you can turn off FaceTime either by choosing FaceTime ⇨ Turn FaceTime Off, or by pressing ⌘+K.

Now when people try to call you using FaceTime, they see a message saying that you're "not available for FaceTime."

# How Do I Keep MacBook Air Running Smoothly?

Unlike almost any other computer on the planet, MacBook Air just works; and it is far less likely to head south on you than most. However, all computers are complex beasts, and MacBook Air is as complex as they come. Its excellent design and engineering ensure a mostly trouble-free operation, but it doesn't hurt to do a little preventive maintenance. The techniques addressed in this chapter help ensure that MacBook Air and the precious data it holds are far less likely to run into trouble.

# Routine MacBook Air Maintenance

Get your maintenance chores off to a solid start by examining a few tasks that I describe as routine — meaning you ought to perform them regularly to help keep MacBook Air running smoothly.

## Emptying the Trash

You might not give a whole lot of thought to the Trash icon that's a permanent resident on the right edge of the Dock. You delete something, MacBook Air dutifully tosses it into the Trash, and you move on with your life.

However, while you're busy with other things, the Trash is slowly expanding with each new deleted file or folder. After a while, the Trash might contain several gigabytes of data. What's the big deal, right? It's just the Trash for goodness sake! Ah, but the Trash is actually a folder on your Mac hard drive. It's a hidden folder located at /Users/You/.Trash (where *You* is your user folder name). So the more space the Trash takes up, the less space you have to store episodes of your favorite shows.

To see just how much space the Trash is occupying, follow these steps:

1. **Double-click the Trash icon in the Dock.**

2. **Choose File ⇨ Get Info.** You can also click the Action icon and then click Get Info, or press ⌘+I. The Trash Info window appears.

3. **Read the Size value.**

In Figure 7.1, you can see that the Trash contains a whopping 3.74GB of data.

So it makes sense to empty the Trash relatively often, perhaps once a month or once every two months, depending on how often you delete things. Here's the safe method of taking out the Trash:

1. **Double-click the Trash icon in the Dock.**

2. **Examine the Trash files to make sure there's nothing important that you deleted by accident.**

7.1 The Trash Info window tells you how much hard drive space the Trash is currently using.

**Caution** Examining the contents of the Trash is crucial because once you empty it, you can't turn back the clock — all of those files are permanently deleted and there's nothing you can do to get any of them back.

3. **If you see a file that you don't want deleted, click and drag the file; and then drop it on the desktop for now.** When you finish emptying the Trash, you can figure out where the rescued file is supposed to go.

4. **Choose Finder ⇨ Empty Trash.** You can also click the Empty button or press Shift+⌘+Delete. MacBook Air asks you to confirm.

5. **Click OK.**

**Genius** When you delete a file from the Trash, MacBook Air leaves it on the hard drive, but tells the system that the file's space is available for use. If you don't like the idea of sensitive files lurking on your drive for who knows how long, choose Finder ⇨ Secure Empty Trash instead. This tells MacBook Air to overwrite each file with gibberish data (see also the section on erasing deleted data in Chapter 9).

Now I don't know about you, but after being so careful about making sure I'm not permanently deleting anything important, it bugs me that my Mac asks if I'm sure I want to go through with it. Of course I'm sure! Fortunately, you can work around this annoyance in a couple of ways.

The easiest is to hold down the Option key while you choose Finder ⇨ Empty Trash or click the Empty button. If your fingers are limber enough, you can also press Option+Shift+⌘+Delete.

A more long-term solution is to tell MacBook Air not to bother with the confirmation message at all. Here are the steps to follow to turn off this message:

1. **In any Finder window, choose Finder ⇨ Preferences.** The Finder Preferences window appears.

2. **Click the Advanced icon.**

**Genius** If you find that you regularly use the Secure Empty Trash command, you can configure Finder to always empty the Trash securely. Follow Steps 1 and 2 to display the Advanced tab of the Finder Preferences dialog, and then select the Empty Trash Securely check box.

3. **Deselect the Show warning before emptying the Trash check box, as shown in Figure 7.2.** You can also select the Empty Trash securely check box to force MacBook Air to always overwrite files with gibberish data when you remove them from the Trash.

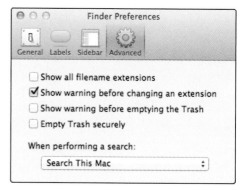

# Cleaning up your desktop

The Mac desktop is a handy place to store things, and most Mac users aren't shy about doing just that, so they end up with dozens of

7.2 To get rid of MacBook Air's Trash confirmation prompts, deselect the Show warning before emptying the Trash check box.

icons scattered around the desktop. This isn't a terrible thing, to be sure, but it's also not very efficient. Once you have more than, say, a dozen icons on your desktop, finding the one you want becomes a real icon-needle-in-a-desktop-haystack exercise.

So, periodically (about once every couple of weeks), you should tidy up your desktop so that you can find things easily and keep the desktop a useful tool. You can do a couple of things:

1. **Get rid of any icons you absolutely don't need on the desktop.**

   - If you're still using the icon, move it to the appropriate folder in your user account.

   - If you don't need the icon anymore, off to the Trash it goes.

2. **Organize the remaining icons.**

   - If you just want to organize the icons by name, click the desktop and then choose View ⇨ Sort By ⇨ Name (or press Control+Option+⌘+1).

   - If you want the icons sorted and aligned, click the desktop and then choose View ⇨ Clean Up By ⇨ Name (or press Option+⌘+1). This command lines up all the icons in neat columns and rows based on the desktop's invisible grid, and sorts the icons by name.

   - If you want to apply a label to related icons, select them, right-click the selection, and then click a label color. You can then sort the icons by label: Click the desktop and then choose View ⇨ Clean Up By ⇨ Label (or press Option+⌘+7).

# Deleting unneeded files

I mentioned earlier that a neglected Trash folder can eat up a lot of hard drive real estate. If you're minding MacBook Air's hard drive and you find that you're running low on free space, you should empty the Trash as a first step. You should also uninstall any programs you no longer use, as described in the next section.

Other than that, I suggest periodically rummaging through the folders in your user account to look for documents, downloads, and other files that you don't need. It's a good idea to sort the files by size (choose View ⇨ Arrange By ⇨ Size, or press Option+⌘+6) so that you can start by deleting the largest files you no longer use. Send these items to the Trash, and when you're done empty the Trash to recover the hard drive space. However, you should also consider backing up your system before you start trashing a lot of files.

**Caution** When deleting files, all folders in your user account are fair game, except for the Library folder (~/Library). Messing with the wrong files in this folder can cause MacBook Air, or your programs, to behave erratically or crash. Therefore, I highly recommend leaving the Library folder alone when purging old files.

# Uninstalling unused applications

To free up some room on MacBook Air's hard drive, get rid of any installed applications that you no longer use. The great thing about uninstalling Mac software is that it's just so darn easy. If you've ever used Windows, you know that removing a program is a long, involved process that always requires a large number of mouse clicks. In Mac OS X, however, the uninstall process couldn't be simpler:

- **In Finder, choose the Applications folder.** There's a chance the application you want to delete is in the Utilities folder, so you may need to choose that folder before continuing.

- **If the application comes with an uninstall utility, double-click that program and then follow the instructions that appear on-screen.** Otherwise, click and drag the folder (or icon) of the application you want to delete, and then drop the folder on the Trash.

**Note** Dropping an application's icon on the Trash is the easy way to delete a program, but it's not always the complete way, since the application may leave behind a preferences file as well as files in the Library folder. A utility such as App Delete (www.reggieashworth.com/appdelete) can get rid of these stray files.

# Setting the software update schedule

One of the most important things you can do to keep MacBook Air in the pink is to update its system software and applications. Apple is constantly improving its software by fixing bugs, adding features, closing security holes, and improving performance. So the MacBook Air software will always be in top shape if you install these updates regularly.

The good news is that MacBook Air checks for updates automatically. By default, MacBook Air does a weekly check, but you can change that if you'd prefer a shorter or longer schedule. Follow these steps:

1. **Click System Preferences in the Dock.** The System Preferences window appears.

2. **Click Software Update.** The Software Update window opens.

3. **Make sure the Check for updates check box is selected, as shown in Figure 7.3.**

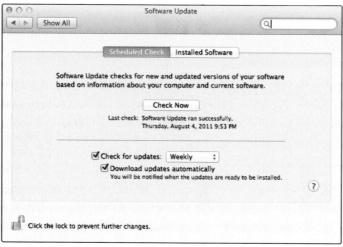

7.3 Select the Check for updates check box and then use the list to choose the update frequency.

4. **Choose the frequency with which you want MacBook Air to check for new updates from the Check for updates list.** Your choices are Daily, Weekly, or Monthly.

# Updating software manually

If you configure Software Update to check for updates weekly or monthly, there may be times when this frequency isn't what you want:

- If MacBook Air is turned off when the time for the next scheduled update occurs, MacBook Air skips that check.

- If someone tells you that an important update is available, you might not want to wait until the next scheduled check to get it.

For these and similar scenarios, you can grab MacBook Air by the scruff of its electronic neck and force it to check for updates. You can do this in two ways:

- Click System Preferences in the Dock, click Software Update, and then click Check Now.

- Click the Apple icon in the menu bar and then click Software Update.

**Genius**

Software Update applies only to Apple software. If you have other software installed on MacBook Air, see if the applications come with update features and, if so, make regular use of them. For example, for Microsoft Office run the Microsoft AutoUpdate application (in Finder, choose Applications ➪ Microsoft AutoUpdate).

# More MacBook Air Maintenance

In addition to maintenance tasks that you should perform frequently to keep MacBook Air in fighting form, there are other maintenance chores you can run. If you really want to get MacBook Air in tip-top shape, perform the tasks outlined in the following sections from time to time.

## Removing login items

When you start MacBook Air, lots of behind-the-scenes tasks are performed to set up the computer for your use. One such task is that MacBook Air checks the list of items that are supposed to start automatically when you log on to your user account. These items are usually applications, but they can also be files, folders, and shared network locations. Appropriately, these items are called login items.

Most login items are added by applications because they need some service running right from the get-go. Typical examples include the following:

- **iTunesHelper.** iTunes uses this application to detect when an iPod, iPhone, or iPad is connected to MacBook Air.

- **iAntiVirus.** This third-party application runs in the background to protect MacBook Air from viruses and other malware.

- **Microsoft Database Daemon.** Microsoft Office uses this application to check for available updates to the Office software.

As you can see, login items are usually quite important. However, not all of them are vital. For example, a login item might be associated with an application you no longer use, or it might open a file or folder that you no longer need at start-up. Whatever the reason, these unneeded login items serve only to slow down MacBook Air's start-up and consume extra system memory. Therefore, from time to time you should check your user account's login items and remove those that you no longer need.

Follow these steps to remove a login item:

1. **Click System Preferences in the Dock.** The System Preferences window opens.

2. **Click Users & Groups.** The Users & Groups preferences window opens.

3. **Click the lock icon.**

4. **Type the name and password of an administrator account and then click Unlock.**

5. **Click the Login Items tab.** You see a list of login items, as shown in Figure 7.4.

6. **Click the login item you want to remove.**

7. **Click the minus sign (–).** MacBook Air removes the login item.

8. **Click the lock icon to prevent further changes in the Accounts preferences window.**

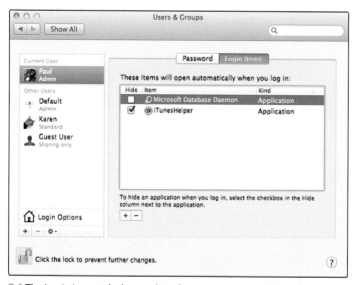

7.4 The Login Items tab shows a list of your user account's login items.

# Cleaning MacBook Air

MacBook Air is a beautiful piece of technology, no doubt about it, but in the long run it's only as good looking as it is clean. Unfortunately, computers never stay clean for long: Screens get fingerprints on them; keyboards collect crumbs and other particles; mice get grimy; and, unless you have some kind of heavy-duty air purifier on the job, all computer parts are world-class dust magnets.

To keep MacBook Air looking sharp, you should give it a thorough cleaning every so often (how often depends on your own cleanliness standards and outside factors such as how dusty your room is). To clean the exterior of MacBook Air, follow these general steps:

1. **Turn off and unplug MacBook Air.**

2. **Use a soft, dry, clean cloth to wipe any excess dust from the screen, keyboard, and mouse.** If you still have it, use the soft, black cloth that came with MacBook Air to do the wiping. If your components are still dirty (fingerprints, smudges, and so on), continue with the remaining steps.

**Caution**

Never spray water or any other liquid on the LCD screen. The liquid could seep into the screen or computer case and damage the electronics.

3. **Take a soft, clean cloth and dampen it with water.** Be sure to merely dampen the cloth — you don't want any excess water to drip on your MacBook Air.

4. **Use the damp cloth to wipe the screen and other components.**

5. **If you see any dust buildup around MacBook Air's ports, use a vacuum with a soft brush attachment to suck up the dust.** While you have the vacuum handy, use it on your keyboard to suck up dust or other particles that have settled between (or even below) the keys.

**Genius**

If water seems too low-tech of a solution (pun intended), give Klear Screen a try. It comes in an Apple version (recommended by Apple itself). The kit contains iKlear, an antistatic screen polish, and a soft chamois cloth. See www.klearscreen.com for more info.

# Preparing for Trouble

You should assume that, at some point, your MacBook Air will have a serious problem, so you should prepare to handle it. Performing regular backups, as I discuss later in this chapter, is a great start, but I also believe you need to do three other things: create a secondary user account with default settings, create a Mac OS X Lion Recovery disk, and create a secondary boot device.

## Creating a secondary user account

MacBook Air lets you define multiple accounts, but if you're the sole user of the computer, you don't need another account, right? True, but having a secondary account around is actually a useful troubleshooting device, as long as you don't customize, tweak, or in any way hack MacBook Air using that account. The idea is that you want the other user account to be pure. That is, an account that uses only the default settings. This way, if MacBook Air starts acting up, you can log in to the secondary account and see if the problem persists. If it doesn't, you know that the problem is almost certainly related to user-specific settings you applied in your main account.

Here are the steps to follow to set up a secondary user account on MacBook Air:

1. **Click System Preferences in the Dock.** The System Preferences window appears.

2. **Click the Users & Groups icon.** The Users & Groups preferences appear.

3. **Click the lock icon, type MacBook Air's administrator credentials, and then click OK.**

4. **Click Add a user account (the + icon).**

5. **In the New Account list, choose Administrator.**

6. **Use the Name text box to type the account name.** For example, type Default Account (because this account will use the default settings).

7. **Use the Account name text box to type a short version of the account name.**

8. **Use the Password and Verify text boxes to type a secure password for the account.** Figure 7.5 shows the dialog filled in so far.

7.5 Use this dialog to set up MacBook Air with a secondary administrator account for troubleshooting.

9. **Use the Password hint text box to type a hint about your password, just in case you forget it.**

10. **Click Create User.** System Preferences creates the secondary account.

**Caution**
Because you're creating an all-powerful administrator account, it's really important that you give this account a secure password (and it's just as important that you don't forget it). The password should be at least eight characters long with a mix of uppercase and lowercase letters, numbers, and symbols. Click the key icon beside the Password text box to check the strength of your password (a good password turns the Quality bar all green).

# Creating a Mac OS X Lion Recovery disk

Mac OS X Lion carves out a portion of the MacBook Air hard drive with a separate partition called the Recovery HD. You can use this partition to repair your MacBook Air's hard drive, restore files from a Time Machine backup, and more.

Recovery HD is a welcome new tool, particularly if you're having troubles with your MacBook Air's main hard drive, but it suffers from a glaring problem: If MacBook Air's entire hard drive fails, the Recovery HD fails also. Not good!

To protect yourself from such a scenario, you can create a Recovery disk, which is a USB flash drive or other external hard drive that contains the same tools as the Recovery HD. That way, if your entire MacBook Air hard drive gives up the ghost, you can still access the Recovery tools.

Follow these steps to create a Recovery disk:

1. **Download and install the Recovery Disk Assistant from** http://support.apple.com/kb/DL1433**.**

2. **Connect a USB thumb drive or external hard drive to your MacBook Air.** The drive you use must have a capacity of at least 1GB.

3. **When the Recovery Disk Assistant recognizes the drive, click the drive icon and then click Continue.**

**Caution**
When the Recovery Disk Assistant creates the Recovery disk, it first erases the disk. Therefore, if the disk contains any files you want to preserve, be sure to copy the files to a safe location before proceeding.

4. **Type your MacBook Air administrative password.** The Recovery Disk Assistant creates the disk.

5. **Click Quit.**

# Creating a secondary boot device

If you want to paint the exterior of your house or wash the outside windows, you can't do either job from inside. This is analogous to performing certain troubleshooting tasks with MacBook Air, such a repairing the hard drive (described later in this book). You can't fix the drive while the Mac operating system is using it. Instead, you have to "step outside" of the MacBook Air hard drive to repair it. How do you do that? By creating a secondary boot device that you can boot to instead of the internal MacBook Air hard drive.

You can do this in several ways, but the following are the most common:

- **The Mac OS X Lion Recovery HD or Recovery disk.** This is the easiest way to go because the Recovery HD is already set up and loaded with tools. Be sure to also create a separate Recovery disk, as described in the previous section, just in case the Recovery HD is inaccessible.

- **Another Mac connected by a Thunderbolt cable.** You can start your Mac in target disk mode, as described in Chapter 10, and then its hard drive appears as a drive on the other Mac. This enables you to use Disk Utility on the other Mac to verify or repair your Mac's hard drive. This is the way to go if you can't access the Recovery HD and you don't have a separate Recovery disk.

# Backing up MacBook Air

The data you create on MacBook Air is as precious as gold, not only because it's yours, but mostly because it's simply irreplaceable. Macs are reliable machines, but they do crash and all hard drives eventually die. At some point your data will be at risk. To avoid losing that data forever, you need to back up MacBook Air early and often.

Fortunately, MacBook Air comes with Time Machine, a backup application unlike anything you've seen before in the Mac world:

- **The initial Time Machine backup includes your entire Mac.**

- **Time Machine runs another backup every hour.** This one includes only those files and folders that you've changed or created since the most recent hourly backup.

- **Time Machine runs a daily backup.** It includes only those files and folders that you've changed or created since the most recent daily backup.

- **Time Machine runs a weekly backup.** It includes only those files and folders that you've changed or created since the most recent weekly backup.

- **You can remotely run Time Machine through Apple's Time Capsule.**

All of this is completely automated — Time Machine is a set-it-and-forget-it deal, which is exactly what you want in a backup application. However, Time Machine doesn't stop there — it also keeps old backups. Time Machine stores:

- **The past 24 hourly backups.**

- **All daily backups from the previous month.**

- **All weekly backups until the backup location is full.** It then begins deleting the oldest backups to make room for more.

Keeping these old backups is what gives Time Machine its name. It enables you to go back in time and restore not just a file, but also a version of a file. For example, say on Monday you created a document and added some text, and then spent Tuesday editing that text. If, on Friday, you realize that during Tuesday's edits you deleted some original text that you'd give your eyeteeth to get back, there's no problem. Simply restore the version from Monday.

Time Machine is so simple and so potentially useful that you really ought to make it part of your backup toolkit. If there's a downside to Time Machine, it's that it backs up only to a second hard drive connected to MacBook Air. You can't, say, back up to a network folder. If you want to back up to a network, you need to get Apple's Time Capsule device (see www.apple.com/timecapsule).

When you first connect an external USB or FireWire hard drive, Time Machine sits up and takes notice. It also most likely displays the dialog shown in Figure 7.6. If you want to use the hard drive for your Time Machine backups, click Use as Backup Disk. Otherwise, click Cancel to move on without configuring anything.

7.6 Time Machine usually asks if you want to use a freshly connected hard drive as the backup drive.

If you didn't set up an external hard drive as the Time Machine backup drive, or if you want to use a different external drive as the backup, you can choose the drive by hand, as shown in the following steps:

1. **Click the System Preferences in the Dock.**

2. **Click Time Machine.** If you've never set up a backup drive, the dialog in Figure 7.7 appears.

7.7 You see this dialog if you've never configured Time Machine with a backup drive.

3. **Click Select Disk.** Time Machine displays a list of the hard drives, partitions, and network drives that you can use for backups, as shown in Figure 7.8.

4. **Select the hard drive you want to use.**

5. **Click Use Backup Disk.** If the hard drive has data on it, or if it has never been formatted, Time Machine warns you that it must erase (that is, format) the drive.

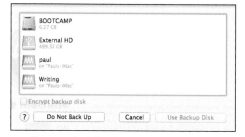

7.8 Choose which hard drive you want Time Machine to use for its backups.

6. **Click Erase.** If you want to save the hard drive's data first, click Choose Another Disk. Copy the drive data to another location, and then repeat this procedure.

When you get back to the Time Machine preferences window, you see that the Time Machine setting is set to ON. The application immediately begins a 120-second countdown to the next backup. If you don't want the backup to run right away, click the X icon beside the countdown.

When you launch Time Machine preferences from now on, it shows you the current status (ON or OFF), how much space is left on the backup drive, and the dates and times of your oldest and most recent backups, as shown in Figure 7.9.

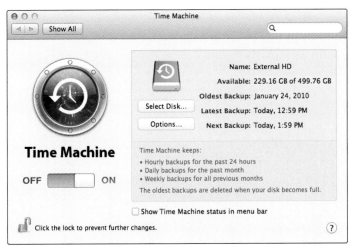

**7.9** The Time Machine window shows the backup device, its free space, and the dates of your oldest and newest backups.

The more data you have, the longer the initial backup takes. If you have data that you don't want included in your backups — such as recorded TV shows you'll delete after watching — it's a good idea to exclude those folders or files. Here's how it's done:

1. **In the Time Machine window, click Options.** Time Machine displays a list of items to exclude from the backups. (At first, this list includes the hard drive that Time Machine is using for the backups, which just makes sense.)

2. **Click the plus sign (+).**

3. **Choose the folder or file that you want to exclude from the backups.**

4. **Click Exclude.** Time Machine adds the folder or file to the Exclude these items from backups list, as shown in Figure 7.10.

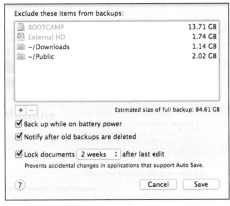

**7.10** You can tell Time Machine to exclude certain folders or files from the backups.

5. **Follow Steps 2 through 4 to exclude any other folders and files that you don't want backed up.**

6. **Click Done.**

**Genius**

If you exclude any items while a backup is running, Time Machine cancels the current backup and reschedules it. If you'd really prefer that the backup run right away, click Select Disk, click the current backup device, and then click Do Not Back Up. Click Select Disk again, choose the hard drive you're using for backups, and then click Use Backup Disk. Time Machine then runs the backup after the 120-second countdown.

# Restoring MacBook Air

If you delete a file by accident, you can always open the Trash to drag it back out. However, there are plenty of situations where recovering a file just isn't possible.

- **You delete the file and then empty the Trash.**

- **You overwrite the file with another file of the same name.** If you notice the problem right away, you can choose Edit ⇨ Undo or press ⌘+Z to undo the file operation. If you don't notice until later, you're stuck.

- **Your hard drive develops a problem that corrupts the file.**

- **You make and save substantial edits to the file.**

The good news is that if you've had Time Machine on the job for a while, you can probably go back in time, locate a version of the file, and then restore it to its original location. Time Machine even lets you keep the existing file if you still need the newer version. Note that I'm talking here about files, but you can also recover folders and even your entire hard drive.

## Restoring files using Time Machine

Follow these steps to restore data from your Time Machine backups:

1. **Use Finder to choose the folder or file that you want to restore.** If you want to restore your entire hard drive, choose Macintosh HD in the sidebar.

**Genius**

In many cases, it's faster to run a Spotlight search on the name of the folder or file you want to restore. In the search results, click the folder or file.

2. **Click the Time Machine icon in the Dock.** The Time Machine interface appears, as shown in Figure 7.11:

3. **Navigate to the version you want by using any of the following techniques (the date and time of the backup appear at the bottom of the screen).**

   - **Click the top arrow to jump to the earliest version.** Click the bottom arrow to return to the most recent version.

   - **Hold down the ⌘ key and click the arrows to navigate through the backups one version at a time.**

   - **Use the timeline to click a specific version.**

   - **Click the version windows.**

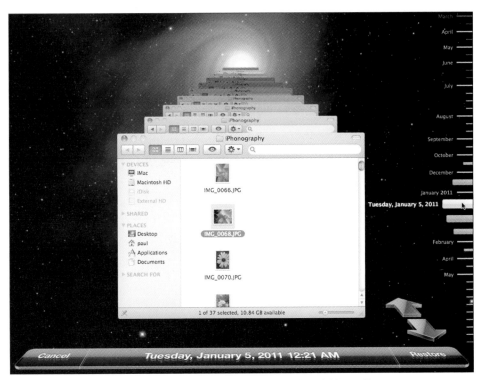

**7.11** Use the Time Machine interface to choose which version of the folder or file you want to restore.

4. **Click the file and click Restore to restore a file.** Time Machine copies the version of the folder or file back to its original location. If the location already contains a folder or file with the same name, you see the Copy dialog shown in Figure 7.12.

5. **Click one of the following buttons:**

- **Keep Original.** Cancels the restore and leaves the existing folder or file as is.

- **Keep Both.** Restores the folder or file and keeps the existing folder or file as is. In this case, Time Machine restores the folder or file and adds the text (original) to the folder or filename.

7.12 The Copy dialog appears if the restore location already has a folder or file with the same name.

- **Replace.** Click this button to overwrite the existing folder or file with the restored folder or file.

## Restoring your system

If disaster strikes and you can't start MacBook Air, you need to restore your system to an earlier state when it was working properly. Here's how you do this using Time Machine:

1. **If you're using a version of Mac OS X prior to Lion, insert your Mac's Install DVD or USB flash drive.**

2. **Turn on or restart your Mac.**

3. **Hold down the Option key while your Mac is restarting.** Your Mac displays a list of start-up disks.

4. **In Mac OS X Lion, double-click Recovery HD.** For earlier versions of Mac OS X, double click the Install DVD or flash drive, and then click the Continue arrow.

5. **In Mac OS X Lion, click Restore From Time Machine Backup and then click Continue.** In earlier versions of Mac OS X, choose Utilities ⇨ Restore System from Backup. The Restore Your System window appears.

6. **Click Continue.** The Select a Backup Source window appears.

7. **Click the hard drive that contains your Time Machine backups.**

8. **Click Continue.** The Select a Backup window appears.

9. **Click the backup you want to use for the restore.**

10. **Click Continue.** The Select a Destination window appears.

11. **Click Macintosh HD.**

12. **Click Restore.** Install Mac OS X begins restoring your system.

# How Do I Maintain the Battery?

A desktop Mac requires a nearby AC outlet, but MacBook Air is capable of running off its internal battery for those times when AC is nowhere in sight. This enables you to use MacBook Air almost anywhere, including a coffee shop, taxi, airplane, and even at the park. However, to make the most out of this portability, you need to take good care of the MacBook Air battery. This includes tracking battery usage, saving as much energy as possible when you're on battery power, periodically reconditioning the battery, and (if you have an original MacBook Air) replacing it at the end of its life cycle. This chapter shows you how to perform all of these battery-related chores.

# Understanding the MacBook Air Battery

Like all Apple notebook computers, MacBook Air comes with an internal battery that enables you to operate the computer without an electrical outlet. Handily, the battery also serves as a backup source of power should the electricity fail.

Older notebook computers used rechargeable nickel metal hydride (NiMH) or nickel cadmium (NiCad) batteries. The NiMH and NiCad types are being phased out because they can suffer from a problem called the memory effect, where the battery loses capacity if you repeatedly recharge it without first fully discharging it.

More recent Mac notebooks used a rechargeable lithium-ion (Li-ion) battery. Li-ion batteries are lighter and last longer than NiMH and NiCad batteries. Most importantly, though, Li-ion batteries don't suffer from the memory effect.

MacBook Air uses a rechargeable lithium-polymer (LiPo or Li-Poly) battery that, as you can see in Figure 8.1 (which shows the fourth-generation MacBook Air), is spread out into four sections to keep the entire battery assembly as thin as possible. A LiPo battery is a variation on the lithium-ion battery. It is generally smaller and lighter than a Li-ion battery, and has about the same capacity.

**Genius** If you just bought your MacBook Air, run it on AC power at first until the battery is fully charged. You'll know the battery is charged when the light on the AC power adapter's connector turns from orange to green. Let MacBook Air run fully charged for at least two hours, then cycle the battery as described later in this chapter.

MacBook Air battery

8.1 MacBook Air's lithium-polymer battery.

# Tracking Battery Usage

When you make the switch from AC to battery with MacBook Air, it's vital to keep an eye on the battery status. Your biggest concern is to prevent MacBook Air from completely discharging the battery while you're working. This can have disastrous consequences because MacBook Air simply shuts down without warning when the battery runs out of juice. If you have unsaved work in any running applications, that work will be lost forever. Tracking the battery usage also helps when you're cycling the MacBook Air battery (as described later in this chapter) and when you want to store MacBook Air for a long time (see the sidebar, a bit later in this section).

The basic tool for tracking battery usage is the battery status icon in the menu bar. If you don't see this icon (it's shaped like a battery), follow these steps to display it:

1. **Choose Apple ⇨ System Preferences.** You can also click the Dock's System Preferences icon. The System Preferences window appears.

2. **Click Energy Saver.** The Energy Saver preferences appear.

3. **Select the Show battery status in the menu bar check box.** MacBook Air adds the battery status icon to the menu bar.

The battery status icon changes to reflect MacBook Air's current power source (AC or battery). When MacBook Air is running on battery power, the amount of black inside the icon tells you the amount of power you have left (see Figure 8.2).

If you want to know how much time you have left before the battery runs out, click the battery status icon. As you can see in Figure 8.3, the menu that appears shows the number of hours and minutes you have left.

8.2 When your MacBook Air is running on battery power, the battery status icon changes to a battery.

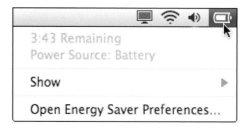

8.3 Click the battery status icon to see the hours and minutes you have remaining on battery power.

**Note**

The amount of battery power remaining is an estimate that MacBook Air calculates based on the your current power consumption, including the applications you have open, the devices you have connected to MacBook Air, and the energy settings you've selected.

## Long-term Storage Considerations

If you know you won't be using MacBook Air for six months or more, you need to consider the effect that this long layoff will have on the battery. You have to guard against two things: losing overall battery capacity and losing the ability to hold a charge. You may lose overall battery capacity if you fully charge the battery before the long layoff. The trickle that the battery slowly loses over time from a full charge will reduce the capacity of the battery and shorten its life. Therefore, you should never fully charge the battery before a long period of idle time. Similarly, if the battery doesn't have much charge before the long layoff, the trickle that it loses may cause the battery to completely discharge. This could result in what's known as a *deep discharge state*, which usually means the battery will no longer hold a charge. To prevent these two problems, it's best to charge the battery to about 50 percent capacity before a long layoff.

Rather than clicking the battery status icon to see the time remaining, or estimating the percentage of battery power you have left based on the state of the battery status icon, you can configure MacBook Air to show either the time or the percentage remaining. Here are the steps to follow:

1. **Click the battery status icon.**

2. **Click Show.**

3. **Click one of the following commands:**

   - **Icon Only.** Click this command to revert to showing just the battery status icon.

   - **Time.** Click this command to see the hours and minutes of battery power remaining.

   - **Percentage.** Click this command to see the percentage of battery power remaining, as shown in Figure 8.4.

8.4 Click the battery status icon in the menu bar, and then click the Percentage command to track remaining battery power.

# Saving Energy When Using Battery Power

We've all been there. You have a long flight ahead of you and your presentation needs work. Unless the plane has an available AC outlet, you need MacBook Air to last a big chunk of that time running on battery power. What are the chances of that happening?

**Genius**

Check out www.seatguru.com to see if the airplane your airline is using has AC near your seat.

Here's the short answer: It depends.

Here's the slightly longer (and more satisfying) answer: It depends on which model of MacBook Air you're using and what you'll be doing with it. Third- and fourth-generation MacBook Airs get between 5 (for the 11-inch model) and 7 (for the 13-inch model) hours per charge under normal use. Count on less (often much less) than 4 hours for earlier versions. However, you can boost all of these numbers by taking steps to minimize MacBook Air's power consumption and thereby maximize its battery life.

The good news is that MacBook Air offers a number of features and techniques that you can use to save energy while running on battery power. By using these features diligently, you can maximize battery power and get that presentation finished.

**Note**

It's an unfortunate fact of life that running MacBook Air on batteries is always a trade-off between battery life and computer performance. The more diligent you are about preserving battery life, the slower MacBook Air will operate.

## Optimizing the MacBook Air energy settings

MacBook Air comes with energy settings that control the battery life/performance trade-off. In this case, you want to adjust those settings so that they favor battery life over performance. The following steps show you how to do that:

1. **Click the battery status icon in the menu bar, and then click Open Energy Saver Preferences.** The Energy Saver window appears. Note that this window is part of System Preferences, so you can also display it by running System Preferences and then clicking the Energy Saver icon.

2. **Click the Battery tab, shown in Figure 8.5.**

Energy Saver

Show All

Battery | Power Adapter

Computer sleep:
1 min    15 min    1 hr    3 hrs  Never

Display sleep:
1 min    15 min    1 hr    3 hrs  Never

☑ Put the hard disk(s) to sleep when possible
☐ Slightly dim the display when using this power source
☑ Automatically reduce brightness before display goes to sleep
☐ Restart automatically if the computer freezes

Current battery charge: 91% Estimated time remaining: 4:01    Restore Defaults

☑ Show battery status in menu bar    Schedule...

Click the lock to prevent further changes.

8.5 In the Energy Saver preferences, use the Battery tab to adjust the battery settings.

3. **The default settings should work fine in most cases, but you might make some adjustments depending on the battery life/performance trade-offs that suit your working style:**

- **Computer sleep.** By default, this slider is set to 10 minutes for battery power. If you want to eke out even more battery life, choose a shorter period of inactivity. If you want to wait for MacBook Air to wake up less often, choose a longer period of inactivity.

- **Display sleep.** By default, this slider is set to 2 minutes for battery power. If you need to study information on the screen, choose a longer period of inactivity so the display doesn't go to sleep as often.

- **Put the hard disk(s) to sleep when possible.** By default, this check box is selected. It means that MacBook Air puts its hard drive to sleep whenever it detects that the drive has not been used for 10 minutes. If you deselect this check box, MacBook Air still puts the hard drive to sleep, but only after 3 hours of inactivity.

- **Slightly dim the display when using this power source.** Select this check box to have Mac OS X reduce the display brightness while MacBook Air is running on battery power. This saves a bit of energy while still keeping the screen readable.

159

- **Automatically reduce brightness before display goes to sleep.** Select this check box to have Mac OS X reduce the screen brightness a few seconds before it puts the display into sleep mode. This sounds annoying, but it's actually quite useful because it serves as a warning when your MacBook Air display is about to sleep. If you want to keep the screen awake, move the mouse pointer or press Shift to prevent the screen from sleeping.

- **Restart automatically if the computer freezes.** Select this check box to have your MacBook Air reboot automatically if the system hangs. It's probably best to leave this option deselected because if your MacBook Air hangs while you're not around, having it restart automatically means it could use battery power unnecessarily.

**Genius**

To set the number of minutes MacBook Air waits before putting an idle hard drive to sleep, choose Finder ➪ Applications ➪ Utilities ➪ Terminal to open a new Terminal session. Type **sudo pmset disksleep** *minutes* (where *minutes* is the number of idle minutes MacBook Air waits before putting the hard drive to sleep). To put the hard drive to sleep after 60 idle minutes, you'd type **sudo pmset disksleep 60**. Note that you must type your MacBook Air administrative password to put this command into effect.

## More ways to save energy

Even with the energy settings optimized for longer battery life, you can still do a few other things to keep MacBook Air running longer. Generally, this means turning off or closing anything you don't need while running on battery power. Here are some suggestions:

- **Quit any unneeded applications.** Running programs may still use up some processor cycles, even when you're not actively using them. For example, your email program may check for new messages every so often. To avoid these power drains, you should shut down any application unnecessary for your work.

- **Minimize your tasks.** Avoid secondary chores, such as checking for software updates and organizing your iTunes library. If your only goal is to finish your presentation, stick to that until it's done (given that you don't know how much time you'll have).

- **Sleep MacBook Air by hand, if necessary.** If you get interrupted — for example, the in-flight meal arrives — don't wait for MacBook Air to put itself to sleep because those few minutes will use up precious battery time. Instead, put MacBook Air to sleep manually right away by either closing the lid or choosing Apple ➪ Sleep (you can also press Option+⌘+Eject).

- **Disconnect any devices you don't need.** Even an unused device can drain battery power, so if you have anything connected to a MacBook Air USB port, disconnect it.

- **If you have an external DVD drive connected to MacBook Air, eject the disc.** Even if you don't use the disc, the DVD drive still occasionally spins up to read something from it, which drains battery power. Eject the disc or, better yet, disconnect the external DVD drive if you don't need it.

- **Turn off AirPort if you don't need it.** When AirPort is on, it regularly checks for available wireless networks, which drains the battery. If you don't need to connect to a wireless network, turn off AirPort to conserve energy. Click the AirPort status icon in the menu bar and then click Turn AirPort Off. If the AirPort status icon isn't displayed, open System Preferences and click Network. Click AirPort and then click Turn AirPort Off.

- **Turn off Bluetooth if you don't need it.** When Bluetooth is running, it constantly checks for nearby Bluetooth devices and this drains the battery. If you aren't using any Bluetooth devices, turn off Bluetooth to save energy. Click the Bluetooth status icon in the menu bar and then click Turn Bluetooth Off. If the Bluetooth status icon isn't displayed, open System Preferences and click Bluetooth. Then deselect the On check box.

- **Use simple applications to accomplish simple tasks.** For example, if you're just typing a to-do list, you don't need to fire up Microsoft Word — use TextEdit instead.

# Cycling the MacBook Air Battery

The MacBook Air lithium-polymer battery doesn't suffer from the memory effect. This means you can run MacBook Air on battery power for as long as you want — 2 seconds, 2 minutes, 2 hours, or whatever you need (within the confines of the battery's capacity, naturally). However, all lithium-based batteries slowly lose their charging capacity over time. You might be able to run MacBook Air on batteries for 4 hours today. However, later on you'll only be able to run the computer for 3 hours on a full charge.

You can't stop this process, but you can delay it significantly by periodically cycling the MacBook Air battery. Cycling — also called reconditioning or recalibrating — a battery means letting it completely discharge and then fully recharging it again. To maintain optimal performance, you should cycle your Mac's battery once every two months or so.

Before getting to the steps, bear in mind that properly cycling the MacBook Air battery includes leaving the computer off for several hours. Therefore, cycle the battery only at a time when leaving it turned off won't be a problem.

**Genius** Paradoxically, the less you use MacBook Air, the more often you should cycle its battery. If you often go several days, or even a week or two without using MacBook Air, you should cycle its battery at least once a month.

Follow these steps to cycle the MacBook Air battery:

1. **Make sure the MacBook Air battery is fully charged.** That is, either make sure that the battery status icon shows 100 percent when you display the percentage, or check that the light on the AC power connector is green. If the status is less than 100 percent or the light is orange, leave MacBook Air plugged in until the battery is fully charged.

**Note** Sometimes the MacBook Air battery shows a battery status of 99 percent and never reaches 100 percent. If the AC connector light shows green, go ahead and treat the battery as fully charged.

2. **Leave MacBook Air in this fully charged state for at least 2 hours.**

3. **Disconnect the MacBook Air AC power connector.** MacBook Air is now running on battery power.

4. **Operate MacBook Air normally by running applications, working with documents, and so on.** When the battery status reaches 5 percent, your Mac warns you that it's now running on reserve power, as shown in Figure 8.6.

> **You are now running on reserve battery power.**
> Please connect your computer to AC power. If you do not, your computer will go to sleep in a few minutes to preserve the contents of memory.
>
> OK

8.6 When the remaining battery power reaches 5 percent, MacBook Air warns you that it's running on reserve power.

5. **Click OK.**

6. **Close all your running documents and applications.**

7. **Either turn MacBook Air off or allow it to switch into sleep mode.**

8. **Leave MacBook Air turned off or sleeping for at least 5 hours.**

9. **Reattach the power cord.**

10. **Turn on MacBook Air and leave the AC cable attached until the battery is fully charged.** It's best to leave MacBook Air in its fully charged state for at least 2 hours.

Apple claims that its notebook batteries are designed to keep up to 80 percent of their original charge even after 300 cycles.

# Replacing the Battery

If your MacBook Air's battery won't charge, or if it runs down very quickly when you're running without outlet power, it's time to yank out the old battery and replace it with a new one. On other Apple notebooks, such as the PowerBook, iBook, MacBook, or MacBook Pro, the battery is what Apple describes as a user-installable feature. That's because on all of those models, it's fairly easy to remove the existing battery and replace it with a new one. They all include some kind of latch or lock that you can easily release to get at the battery.

Unfortunately, that's not the case with MacBook Air, which doesn't come with a battery-release mechanism. Instead, you must remove either 15 or 19 (depending on your version of MacBook Air) screws to get at and release the battery. It's not exactly something routine you'll do on the morning train, but it's not difficult either — just tedious.

## Working with a third- or fourth-generation MacBook Air

Actually, I should say that it's not difficult if you have a first- (2008) or second-generation (early 2010) MacBook Air. I'll show you how to replace the battery in those versions in the next section.

Things are quite a bit trickier with the third-generation (late 2010) and fourth-generation (mid-2011) MacBook Air. That's because Apple decided to secure the case with ten so-called *tamper-proof* (or sometimes *security*) Torx screws. These differ from regular Torx screws because they have a small metal bump in the middle. This prevents a regular Torx screwdriver from seating properly within the screw. So, the only way to remove a third- or fourth-generation MacBook Air case is to use a Torx screwdriver designed to work with tamperproof Torx screws.

Because screwdrivers that can work with tamperproof Torx screws are often hard to find and because, as I write this, it's devilishly difficult to get a replacement battery for these models of MacBook Air, I won't go into all of the details.

To get inside the case, you need a T5 Torx tamperproof screwdriver. If you have one, use it to remove the ten Torx screws that secure the case. The third- and fourth-generation MacBook Air battery appears to be divided into several sections, but it's actually just a single battery pack, as shown previously in Figure 8.1. To remove the battery pack, you must first remove five regular Torx T5 screws. Four of these are on the corners of the battery pack and the fifth is in the middle. Carefully, lift up the entire pack, and then gently pull the plastic tab to release the battery connector, as shown in Figure 8.7. Grab the new battery, insert the connector, drop the battery into its slot, and then replace the screws.

**Caution**    Because the third- and fourth- generation MacBook Airs use several different screw lengths, make sure you keep track of which screw goes where. Also, be sure to touch a metal object before opening the case to ground yourself and prevent a discharge of static electricity from damaging any sensitive components inside the case.

8.7 Lift up the battery and then use the plastic tab to pull out the battery connector.

# Working with a first- or second-generation MacBook Air

If you have a first- or second-generation MacBook Air and you have a replacement MacBook Air battery, follow these steps to install it:

1. **If MacBook Air is still running, choose Apple ⇨ Shut Down and then click Shut Down to turn it off.**

2. **Unplug the power cable and anything else connected to MacBook Air.**

3. **Turn MacBook Air upside down and place it on a flat, clean surface.**

4. **Touch something metal to ground yourself.**

**Caution** When changing the battery, it's vital to discharge your body's pent-up static electricity by touching a metal object. Otherwise, the static electricity discharges into MacBook Air and could damage one or more internal components.

5. **Use a #00 Phillips screwdriver to remove the ten screws on the bottom of the MacBook Air case.** Figure 8.8 shows the location of these. Note the locations of the different-length screws.

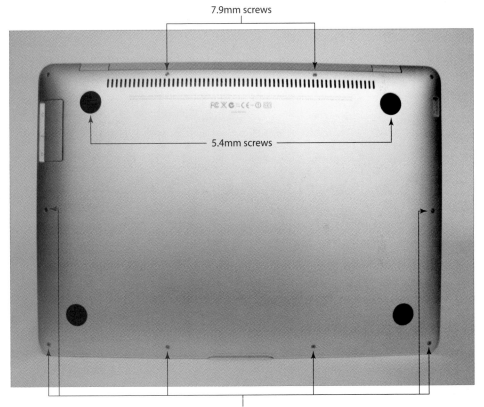

8.8 To open the MacBook Air case, you need to remove ten screws on the bottom.

6. **Carefully lift the bottom off of the MacBook Air case.**

**Caution** Because there are three different screw lengths to worry about, make sure you keep track of which screw goes where. Also, you really do need the teensy #00 Phillips screwdriver (also called a precision or jeweler's screwdriver) for this task. An ordinary #0 Phillips screwdriver isn't small enough.

7. **Use a #00 Phillips screwdriver to remove the nine screws that attach the battery to the chassis.** Figure 8.9 shows the location of these. Note the locations of the different-length screws.

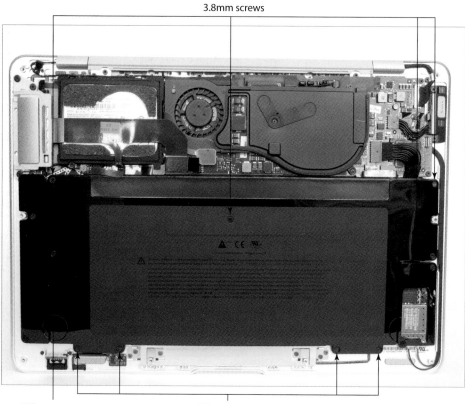

3.8mm screws

7.3mm screws          3.0mm screws

**8.9** To remove the MacBook Air battery, you need to remove the nine screws shown here.

**Note**  You need to dispose of that old battery, of course, so return it to an authorized Apple dealer. Apple is committed to keeping used batteries out of landfills.

8. **Remove the battery connector, as shown in Figure 8.10.**

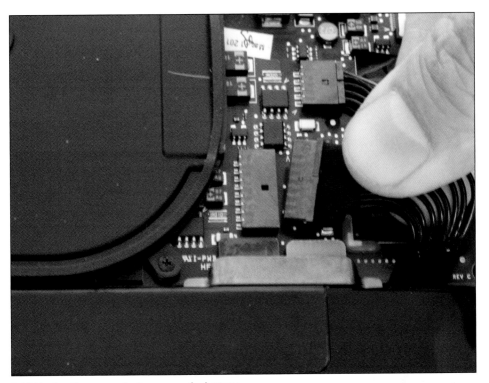

8.10 Unplug the connector to remove the battery.

9. **Plug the new battery into the connector.**

10. **Attach the new battery to the chassis using the nine screws from Step 7.**

11. **Attach the bottom of the MacBook Air case using the ten screws from Step 5.**

**Note**  When replacing the bottom of MacBook Air's case, note that the front edge of the bottom piece has several tabs that fit into the chassis. To get the bottom to sit properly, you must first angle those tabs into the corresponding slots and then lay down the bottom. If the bottom piece isn't flush with the chassis, you may need to snap it into place.

# How Do I Maintain the Hard Drive?

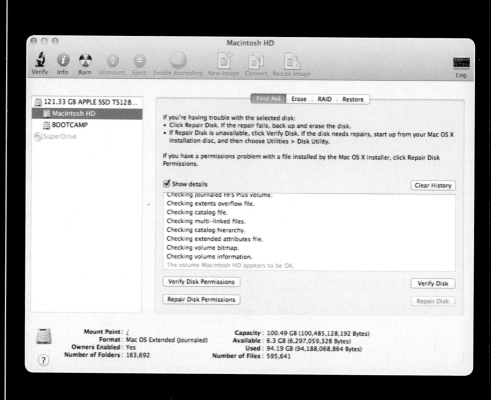

MacBook Air is loaded with important parts, from the screen that lets you see what's going on and the memory that lets you get your work done, to the keyboard that lets you type your two cents' worth. However, if I were forced to pick a MacBook Air MVP (Most Valuable Part), I'd have to go with the hard drive. This crucial component provides a permanent storage area, not only for Mac OS X and your programs, but also, most importantly, for your precious and irreplaceable data. So you want to treat the MacBook Air hard drive right, and that includes using the routine maintenance techniques covered in this chapter.

Although it's true that hard drives are larger than ever these days, it's also true that files are getting larger, too. Music files are almost always multimegabyte affairs. A single half-hour TV show can usurp about 250MB, and movies can be three or four times as large. If you're not careful, it's easy to run out of hard drive space in a hurry.

To prevent that from happening, you should keep an eye on how much free space is left on MacBook Air's hard drive. One way to do this is to open any Finder window and click any folder that resides on the MacBook Air hard drive (such as Desktop, your user folder, or Applications). As you can see in Figure 9.1, Finder displays the amount of available space in the status bar at the bottom of the open window.

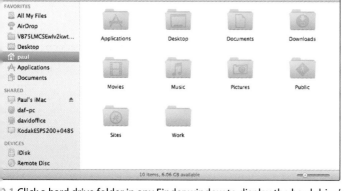

9.1 Click a hard drive folder in any Finder window to display the hard drive's free space in the status bar.

An even better way to keep your eyes peeled for free hard drive space is to configure the desktop to always show this information. Here's how:

1. **Click the desktop.**
2. **Choose Finder ⇨ Preferences.** Your Mac opens the Finder Preferences dialog.
3. **Click the General tab.**

4. **Select the Hard disks check box.**
   Finder displays an icon for your Mac's hard drive on the desktop.

5. **Close the Finder Preferences dialog.**

6. **Choose View ⇨ Show View Options.**
   You can also press ⌘+J. The Desktop window appears.

7. **Select the Show item info check box.**

8. **Click and drag the Icon size slider to 128 × 128, as shown in Figure 9.2.**

Finder now displays extra information under the name of each desktop icon, such as the number of items in a folder and the dimensions of an image. In the case of the Macintosh HD icon, Finder shows the total size of the hard drive and the amount of free space, as shown in Figure 9.3.

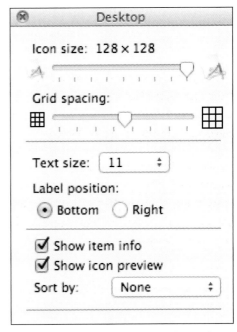

9.2 Select the Show item info check box and increase the Icon size value.

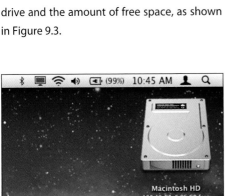

9.3 The Macintosh HD icon now shows the drive's total space and total free space.

# Checking the Hard Drive's Status

A hard drive can suddenly bite the dust thanks to a lightning strike, an accidental drop from a decent height, or an electronic component shorting out. However, most of the time hard drives die a slow death. Along the way, they almost always show some signs of decay, but a hard drive is hidden so how can you see these signs?

Since about 1996, almost all hard-drive manufacturers have built a system called Self-Monitoring Analysis and Reporting Technology (or S.M.A.R.T.) into their drives. This system monitors a number of hard drive parameters, including spin-up time, drive temperature, drive errors, and bad sectors. It monitors these factors over time and looks for signs of impending hard drive failure, including the following:

- The spin-up time gradually slows.
- The drive temperature increases.
- The seek error rate increases.
- The read error rate increases.
- The write error rate increases.
- The number of bad sectors increases.
- An internal consistency check (called the cyclic redundancy check, or CRC) produces an increasing number of errors.

Other factors that might indicate a potential failure are the number of times that the hard drive has been powered up, the number of hours it's been in use, and the number of times the drive has started and stopped spinning. S.M.A.R.T. uses a sophisticated algorithm to combine these attributes into a value that represents the overall health of the drive. When that value goes beyond a predetermined threshold, S.M.A.R.T. issues an alert that hard-drive failure might be imminent.

Although S.M.A.R.T. has been around for awhile and is now standard, taking advantage of its diagnostics originally meant using a third-party program. However, MacBook Air includes a component that can monitor S.M.A.R.T. status and alert you if there's a problem. Here's how to use it:

1. **Click Finder in the Dock.**
2. **Choose Applications ⇨ Utilities ⇨ Disk Utility.** The Disk Utility window appears.

3. **Click MacBook Air's hard drive in the list of drives.**

4. **Read the S.M.A.R.T. Status value, as shown in Figure 9.4.** This is located in the lower-right of the window.

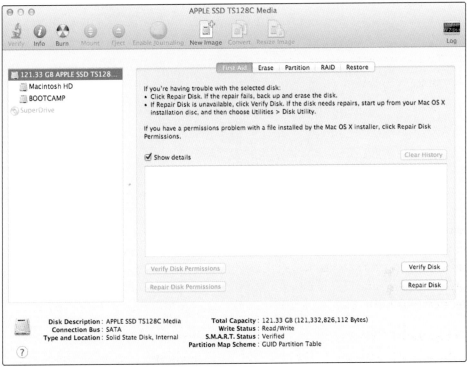

9.4 Check the hard drive's S.M.A.R.T. Status value.

If all is well, the S.M.A.R.T. Status value says Verified. If you see either About to Fail or (worse) Failing (see Figure 9.5), perform an immediate backup. Then replace the hard drive as described later in this chapter.

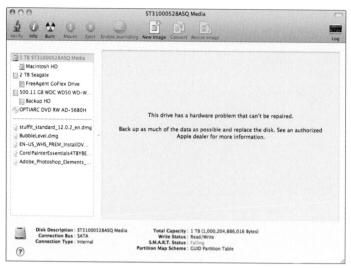

This drive has a hardware problem that can't be repaired.

Back up as much of the data as possible and replace the disk. See an authorized Apple dealer for more information.

Disk Description : ST31000528ASQ Media    Total Capacity : 1 TB (1,000,204,886,016 Bytes)
Connection Bus : SATA    Write Status : Read/Write
Connection Type : Internal    S.M.A.R.T. Status : Failing
Partition Map Scheme : GUID Partition Table

9.5 If the hard drive's S.M.A.R.T. Status value shows Failing, back up your data and then replace the hard drive.

# Verifying the Hard Drive

The S.M.A.R.T. diagnostics (discussed in the previous section) look for catastrophic errors — those that might cause the entire hard drive to go belly up. However, hard drives can also fall prey to smaller maladies that, although they won't cause it to push up daisies, could cause it to behave erratically or even damage files.

For example, MacBook Air maintains what it calls a Catalog file that stores the overall structure of the hard drive, including all of the folders and files. If that file gets corrupted, it might mean that you, or an application, can no longer access a folder or file.

You should check MacBook Air's hard drive for these types of errors every month or so. Here's how:

1. **Click Finder in the Dock.**

2. **Choose Applications ➪ Utilities ➪ Disk Utility.** The Disk Utility window appears.

3. **Click Macintosh HD in the list of drives.**

4. **Click Verify Disk.** Disk Utility warns you that your Mac may slow down or appear to hang during the verification.

5. **Click Verify Disk.** Disk Utility begins the verification check, which takes several minutes.

6. **When the check is complete, read the results, as shown in Figure 9.6.**

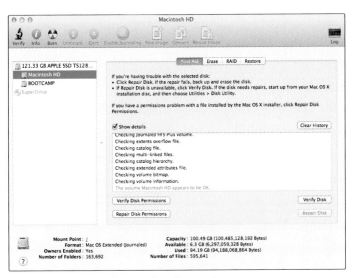

9.6 Check the results of the Verify Disk operation.

7. **There are two possible results:**

   - **No problems.** Say "Whew!" and close Disk Utility.

   - **Problems.** You need to repair the hard drive, as described in Chapter 10.

# Replacing the Hard Drive

Replacing the MacBook Air hard drive is a pretty radical form of maintenance, to be sure! However, no hard drive lasts forever and MacBook Air's is no exception. Use it long enough and often enough, and one day the hard drive will go belly up and you'll need to replace it. As long as you have MacBook Air backed up, as described in Chapter 7, you won't lose any data, and you'll have your computer back on its digital feet in short order.

How hard is it to swap out the old hard drive for a new one? Well, that depends on which version of MacBook Air you're using: a fourth-generation MacBook Air (which came out in late 2011) or an earlier version. The next two sections explain the differences.

# Working with a third- or fourth-generation MacBook Air

As I explain in Chapter 8, doing *anything* inside the case of a third- or fourth-generation MacBook Air is problematic because Apple now uses tamperproof Torx screws to secure the case. Because screwdrivers that work with tamperproof Torx screws (particularly the teensy T5 screws used in the third- and fourth-generation MacBook Air) are often hard to find, and because (as I write this) the flash storage that Apple uses for the third- and fourth-generation hard drive isn't readily available, I won't go into all of the details about replacing the third- and fourth-generation hard drive.

**Note**  Toshiba recently released a new series of flash storage modules called Blade X-gale, which should fit third- and fourth-generation MacBook Airs. These modules come in 64GB, 128GB, and 256GB versions.

Besides a T5 tamperproof screwdriver or bit to remove the ten screws that secure the back of the third- or fourth-generation case, and a regular T5 Torx screwdriver or bit to remove the drive, you also need a hard drive that meets the following specifications:

- **Drive type.** Solid-state flash storage module.
- **Interface.** Mini Serial Advanced Technology Attachment (mSATA).
- **Dimensions.** Width: 24mm; length: 108.9mm; height: 2.2mm.

Follow these steps to install the replacement drive:

1. **Unplug the power cable and anything else connected to MacBook Air.**
2. **Turn MacBook Air upside down and place it on a flat, clean surface.**
3. **Touch something metal to ground yourself.** It's vital to discharge your body's pent-up static electricity by touching a metal object. Otherwise, the static electricity discharges into MacBook Air and could damage one or more internal components.
4. **Use a T5 tamperproof Torx screwdriver to remove the ten screws on the bottom of the MacBook Air case.**

**Caution**  The third- and fourth-generation MacBook Air case uses a couple of different lengths of screws, so make sure you keep track of which screw goes where.

5. **Carefully lift off the bottom of the case.**

6. **Use a T5 Torx screwdriver to remove the single screw that attaches the storage module to the chassis.** Figure 9.7 shows the screw location for the fourth-generation MacBook Air, while Figure 9.8 shows the screw location for the third-generation MacBook Air.

7. **Carefully pull the flash module out of the mSATA connector.**

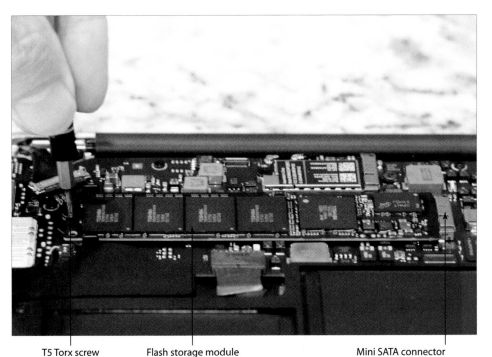

T5 Torx screw          Flash storage module                    Mini SATA connector

9.7 In a fourth-generation MacBook Air, remove the single T5 Torx screw shown here to release the flash module.

8. **Insert the new flash module into the mSATA connector.**

9. **Use a T5 Torx screwdriver to secure the flash module to the chassis.**

10. **Attach the bottom of MacBook Air's case using the ten screws from Step 4.**

177

Mini SATA connector          Flash storage module

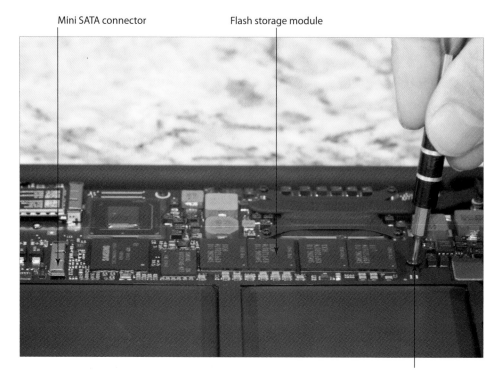

T5 Torx
screw

**9.8** In a third-generation MacBook Air, remove the single T5 Torx screw shown here to release the flash module.

## Working with a first- or second-generation MacBook Air

If you have a first- (2008) or second-generation (early 2010) MacBook Air, you can replace the hard drive without tons of fuss. On the one hand, it's not a trivial exercise, given that the hard drive is safely tucked away inside MacBook Air's case. However, on the other hand, the operation requires no special technical skills. If you can wield a screwdriver without poking yourself in the eye, you'll have no trouble replacing the MacBook Air hard drive.

As you might expect, given the teensy dimensions of the MacBook Air you can't just toss any old hard drive into its cramped insides. In fact, you won't even be able to shoehorn any standard note-book hard drive into a MacBook Air. Instead, you need to look for a special hard drive that meets the following specifications:

- **Form factor.** 1.8 inches wide and 0.2 (5mm) high. This is the only size that fits inside MacBook Air.

- **Drive type.** This can be either a regular hard drive or a solid-state disk.

- **Interface.** Parallel Advanced Technology Attachment (PATA) with a 40-pin ZIF (zero insertion force) connector.

**Caution** Solid-state disks (SSDs) are much more robust than hard disk drives (HDDs). However, SSDs are much more expensive, so watch your budget.

Once you have your replacement hard drive, follow these steps to install it:

1. **In the unlikely event that MacBook Air is still running, choose Apple ⇨ Shut Down and then click Shut Down to turn it off.**

2. **Unplug the power cable and anything else connected to MacBook Air.**

3. **Turn MacBook Air upside down and place it on a flat, clean surface.**

4. **Touch something metal to ground yourself.** It's vital to discharge your body's pent-up static electricity by touching a metal object. Otherwise, the static electricity discharges into MacBook Air and could damage one or more internal components.

5. **Use a #00 Phillips screwdriver to remove the ten screws on the bottom of the MacBook Air case, shown in Figure 9.9.** Note the locations of the different-length screws.

**Caution** After you open MacBook Air's case, note that there are three different screw lengths to worry about, so make sure you keep track of which screw goes where. Also, you really do need the teensy #00 Phillips screwdriver (also called a precision or jeweler's screwdriver) for this task. An ordinary #0 Phillips screwdriver isn't small enough.

6. **Carefully lift off the bottom of the case.**

7. **Remove the connector for the cable that runs from MacBook Air's external ports, as shown in Figure 9.10.**

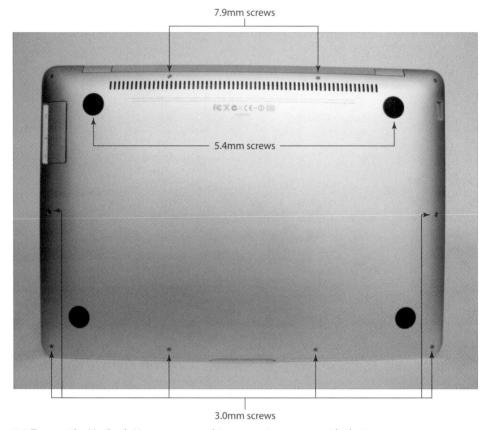

7.9mm screws

5.4mm screws

3.0mm screws

9.9 To open the MacBook Air case, you need to remove ten screws on the bottom.

8. **Use a #00 Phillips screwdriver to remove the four screws that attach the hard drive to the chassis, shown in Figure 9.11.** Here are a couple of notes to bear in mind:

- **You should see a thin, black cable running along the back side of the hard drive (that is, the side closest to the back of MacBook Air).** Carefully loosen that cable from the plastic sheath that holds the hard drive for easier access to the two screws on that side.

- **One of the screws on the back side of the hard drive is covered by a small piece of plastic.** You need to lever that bit of plastic out to access the screw.

9.10 To get to the hard drive, you must first disconnect the cable for the external ports.

9. **Remove the motherboard connector for the hard drive's interface cable, as shown in Figure 9.12.**

10. **Lift the hard drive out and remove it from the plastic bracket.**

11. **Remove the rubber bumper that surrounds the old drive.**

12. **Remove the strip of black tape that helps keep the ZIF connector attached to the hard drive, and then remove the ZIF connector.**

13. **Attach the ZIF connector to the new hard drive.**

3.0mm screws

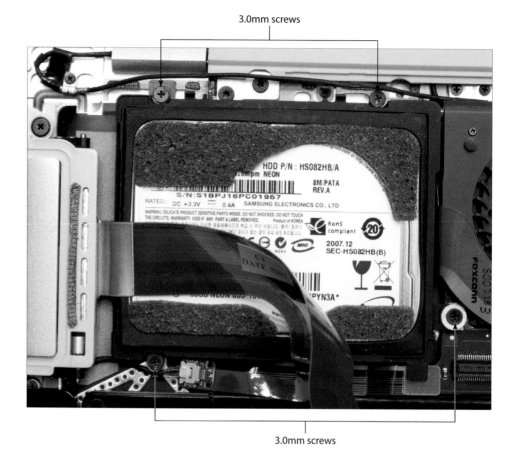

3.0mm screws

9.11 To remove the hard drive, you must remove the four screws that attach it to the chassis.

14. **Place the rubber bumper around the new hard drive.**

15. **Place the new hard drive inside the plastic bracket.**

16. **Attach the motherboard connector on the other end of the hard drive's interface cable.**

17. **Attach the hard drive to the chassis using the four screws from Step 8.**

18. **Attach the connector for the cable that runs from MacBook Air's external ports.**

19. **Attach the bottom of MacBook Air's case using the ten screws from Step 5.**

**9.12** Disconnect the hard drive's interface cable.

With your new hard drive in place, you must now reinstall Mac OS X, as described in Chapter 10. Once you've done that, you can get to your old system by restoring your most recent Time Machine backup.

**Note**

When putting the bottom of the case back on, note that the front edge of the bottom piece has several tabs that fit into the chassis. To get the bottom to sit properly, you must first angle those tabs into the corresponding chassis slots and then lay down the bottom. If the bottom piece isn't flush with the chassis, you may need to snap it into place.

# How Do I Solve
# MacBook Air Problems?

## Mac OS X Utilities

**Restore From Time Machine Backup**
You have a backup of your system that you want to restore.

**Reinstall Mac OS X**
Set up and install a new copy of Lion.

**Get Help Online**
Browse the Apple Support website to find help for your Mac.

**Disk Utility**
Repair or erase a disk using Disk Utility.

Continue

The good news about Mac problems — whether they're software or hardware problems — is that they're relatively rare. The reason for such rarity is a simple one: Application developers and device manufacturers only have to build their Mac products for machines made by a single company. This really simplifies things, and results in fewer problems. Not, however, no problems. Even in a Mac world, applications and devices sometimes behave strangely or not at all. In this chapter, I give you some general troubleshooting techniques for tackling both software and hardware woes.

# General Software Troubleshooting Techniques

One of the ongoing mysteries that all Mac users experience at one time or another is what might be called the "now-you-see-it-now-you-don't" problem. This gremlin plagues you for a while and then mysteriously vanishes without any intervention on your part. (It also tends not to occur when you ask your tech-savvy brother-in-law or someone from the IT department to troubleshoot the problem.) When this happens, most people just shake their heads and resume working, grateful to no longer have to deal with the problem.

## Tracking down the problem

Unfortunately, most computer ills don't just disappear. For more intractable problems, your first order of business is to track down the source of the glitch. There's no easy or set way to go about this, but it can be done if you take a systematic approach. Over the years, I've found that the best approach is to ask a series of questions designed to gather the required information and/or to narrow down what might be the culprit:

- **Did you get an error message?** Unfortunately, most computer error messages are obscure and do little to help you resolve a problem directly. However, error codes and error text can help you down the road, either by giving you something to search for in an online database or by providing information to a tech support person. Therefore, you should always write down the full text of any error message that appears.

**Genius** If the error message is lengthy and you can still use other programs on MacBook Air, don't bother writing down the full message. Instead, while the message is displayed, press Shift+⌘+3 to place an image of the current screen on the desktop. To capture just the error window, press Shift+⌘+4 instead. If you're worried about losing access to the desktop, save the image to a flash drive or print it out.

- **Is there an error message in the Console?** If an error occurs behind the scenes, you don't see anything on-screen to tell you that something's amiss. However, there's a good chance that MacBook Air made a note of the error as a Console message. To check, open Finder and choose Applications ➪ Utilities ➪ Console. You should check both the system log (click system.log in the Log List) and the kernel log (click kernel.log in the Log List; see Figure 10.1). Any message you see is likely to be far too cryptic for mere mortals to decipher, but it will likely make sense to someone in tech support. You can also Google the message text to see if a solution appears online.

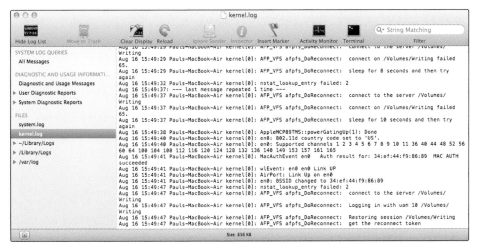

10.1 You can use the Console utility to check for error messages.

- **Did you recently change any application settings?** If so, try reversing the change to see whether doing so solves the problem. If that doesn't help, check the software developer's website to see whether an upgrade or patch is available. Otherwise, you could try uninstalling and then reinstalling the program.

- **Did you recently install a new program?** If you suspect a new program is causing system instability, restart MacBook Air and try operating the system for a while without using the new program. If the program has any login items that load at start-up, be sure to deactivate them (this is covered in Chapter 7). If the problem doesn't reoccur, the new program is likely the culprit. Try using the program without any other programs running. You should also examine the program's README file (if it has one) to look for known problems and possible workarounds.

- **It's also a good idea to check for a version of the program that's compatible with your version of OS X**. For example, some older versions of Mac applications might not be compatible with Lion (OS X 10.7). Again, you can also try reinstalling the program. Similarly, if you recently upgraded an existing program, try uninstalling the upgrade.

**Note**

One common cause of program errors is having one or more program files corrupted because of hard drive errors. Before you reinstall a program, try repairing the Mac's hard drive, as described later in this chapter.

- **Did you recently install a new device?** If you recently installed a new device or if you recently updated an existing device driver, one of these might be causing the problem. Run through the general hardware troubleshooting techniques later in this chapter.

- **Did you recently install any updates?** It's an unfortunate fact of life that occasionally updates designed to fix one problem end up causing another. You can't uninstall a software update, so your only choice is to restore MacBook Air to a previous version.

- **Did you recently change any System Preferences?** If the problem started after you changed MacBook Air's configuration, try reversing the change. Even something as seemingly innocent as activating a screen saver can cause problems, so don't rule anything out.

# Basic software troubleshooting steps

Figuring out the cause of a problem is often the hardest part of troubleshooting, but by itself it doesn't do you much good. When you know the source, you need to parlay that information into a fix for the problem. I discussed a few solutions in the previous section, but here are a few other general fixes you need to keep in mind:

- **Close all programs.** You can often fix flaky behavior by shutting down all of your open programs and starting again. This is a particularly useful fix for problems caused by low memory or low system resources.

- **Log out.** Logging out clears the memory and gives you a slightly cleaner slate than merely closing all your programs. Pull down the Apple menu and choose Log Out *User* (where *User* is your MacBook Air username), or press Shift+⌘+Q to log out quickly.

- **Restart MacBook Air.** If there are problems with some system files and devices, logging out won't help because these objects remain loaded. By restarting MacBook Air, you reload the entire system, which is often enough to solve many problems. I discuss various ways of restarting MacBook Air later in this chapter.

## Monitoring MacBook Air to look for problems

If MacBook Air feels sluggish or an application is behaving erratically, what might the problem be? Perhaps the processor is busy with other tasks; perhaps MacBook Air is running low on memory; or perhaps there's a problem with the hard drive. It could be any of these things, but the only way to tell is to look under the hood, so to speak, and monitor these aspects of MacBook Air.

MacBook Air's monitoring tools are useful troubleshooters, but they're also good for acquainting yourself with MacBook Air. Monitoring things like the processor and memory usage regularly (not just when you have a problem) helps you get a feel for what's normal on MacBook Air, which then helps you better diagnose MacBook Air when you suspect a problem.

## Monitoring CPU usage

The CPU (central processing unit or just processor) is the chip inside MacBook Air that acts as the computer's control and command center. Almost everything you do on MacBook Air and almost everything that happens within MacBook Air goes through the CPU. It is, in short, a pretty darned important component, and it pays to keep an eye on how much MacBook Air's CPU is being taxed by the system. If MacBook Air feels less responsive than usual, or if a program has become very slow, it could be because the CPU is running at or near full speed.

To see if that's the case, you can use Activity Monitor, which gives you a list of everything running on MacBook Air and tells you, among other things, what percentage of the CPU's resources are being used. Follow these steps to get started:

1. **Click Finder in the Dock.** The Finder window opens.

2. **Choose Applications ⇨ Utilities ⇨ Activity Monitor.**

3. **Click the CPU tab at the bottom.**

Figure 10.2 shows the Activity Monitor window. The bulk of the window is taken up by a list of running programs, which Activity Monitor calls processes. A *process* is a running instance of an executable program. All the applications you have running are processes, but so are all of the behind-the-scenes programs that MacBook Air and your applications require to function properly.

10.2 You can use Activity Monitor to keep an eye on MacBook Air's CPU usage.

**Note**

If you happen to have the Console utility still running, you can also click the Activity Monitor command in the toolbar.

**Genius**

In Activity Monitor, processes appear alphabetically by name, but you can change that order by clicking any column header. For example, to sort the processes by CPU usage, click the CPU column header. This gives you an ascending sort; click the header again to get a more useful descending sort.

By default, Activity Monitor shows the processes associated with your user account: the applications you've launched, your user account's login items, and other programs that MacBook Air started when you signed in. However, this is by no means a complete list of the running processes. You can use the Show list to display a different set of processes. Here are the most important items in the Show list:

- **All Processes.** Displays a complete list of all the running processes.

- **All Processes, Hierarchically.** Displays a complete list of all the running processes, as well as the subprocesses that each one has started. This is useful if you suspect (or want to find out if) a particular application is spawning lots of subapplications that are eating up CPU time.

- **My Processes.** Displays the list of processes that are running under your username, as shown in Figure 10.2.

- **System Processes.** Displays the list of processes that were started by Mac OS X (that is, the root user).

- **Other User Processes.** Displays the list of processes that are running under a username other than yours and the root user.

- **Active Processes.** Displays just those processes that are currently using or have recently used the CPU.

- **Inactive Processes.** Displays just those processes that are running, but haven't used the CPU in a while.

- **Windowed Processes.** Displays just those processes associated with running programs that you can see in the Dock (that is, the programs with open windows with which you can interact).

- **Selected Processes.** You can use this item to display specific processes. For example, if you want to watch certain processes, you'd choose them and then choose Selected Processes.

Whichever processes you display, the list itself is divided into a number of columns that give you information about the resources that each process is using. Here's a summary:

- **PID.** This column shows the process identifier, which is a unique numerical value that MacBook Air assigns to the process while it's running.

- **Process Name.** This is the name (usually the executable filename) of the process. You also see the icon for each windowed process.

- **User.** This value tells you the name of the user or service that launched the process.

**Genius** You can control how often Activity Monitor refreshes its data. Choose View ➪ Update Frequency, and then choose Very Often (refreshes the data twice per second); Often (refreshes the data every second); Normally (refreshes the data every 2 seconds — this is the default); or Less Often (refreshes the data every 5 seconds).

- **% CPU.** This is the key column for you in this section. The values here tell you the percentage of CPU resources that each process is using. If your system seems sluggish, look for a process consuming all, or nearly all, of the CPU's resources. Most programs monopolize the CPU occasionally for short periods, but a program stuck at 100 percent for a long time most likely has some kind of problem. In that case, try shutting down the program or process, as described later in this chapter.

- **Threads.** This value tells you the number of threads that each process is using. A *thread* is a program task that can run independently of, and usually concurrently with, other tasks in the same program, in which case the program is said to support multithreading. Multithreading improves program performance, but programs that have an unusually large number of threads can slow down the computer because they have to spend too much time switching from one thread of execution to another.

- **Real Mem.** This value tells you approximately how much memory the process is using. This value is less useful because a process might genuinely require a lot of memory to operate. However, if this value is steadily increasing for a process that you're not using, it could indicate a problem, and you should shut down the process, as described later in this chapter.

- **Kind.** This column shows you the type of CPU on which the process is programmed to run: Intel, Intel 64 bit, or PowerPC (which is no longer supported in Mac OS X Lion, so you won't see any of these).

The bottom part of the Activity Monitor window shows the CPU totals. For the percentage of CPU usage, you see separate percentages for User (processes running under your user account), System (processes that MacBook Air is using), and Idle (the amount of resources available to the CPU) as a percentage of the total.

You want to monitor what percentage of the CPU is currently being used, but it's a hassle to always switch to Activity Monitor to check this. An easier way is to configure the Activity Monitor Dock icon as a graph that shows the current state of the CPU usage value. To do this, choose View ⇨ Dock Icon ⇨ Show CPU Usage. Figure 10.3 shows what it looks like.

Activity Monitor icon

**10.3** You can configure the Activity Monitor Dock icon as a graph that shows the current CPU usage.

## Changing Your Priorities

The priority of a process determines how much scheduling time the CPU gives to it. A higher-priority process runs faster (because it gets more CPU time) and a lower-priority process runs slower. By default, all processes are given the same priority. However, if you want to try changing a process priority (for example, to make the process run faster), choose Finder ⇨ Applications ⇨ Utilities ⇨ Terminal. In the Terminal window, type the following command: **sudo renice *priority PID***.

Here, replace *priority* with a value between –20 (highest priority) and 20 (lowest priority). Replace *PID* with the process identifier number of the process with which you want to work. You'll need to type an administrator's password for this to work.

## Monitoring memory usage

Memory is the lifeblood of any computer, and MacBook Air is no different. If your system runs low on memory, everything slows to a crawl, and programs may mysteriously fail. You can use Activity Monitor to examine how much real and virtual memory each running process is using. However, the total amount of memory being used is important as well. To see that, you must click the System Memory tab in the Activity Monitor window, as shown in Figure 10.4.

**Note** Your computer can address memory beyond what is physically installed on the system. This nonphysical memory is called *virtual memory*, and it's implemented by using a piece of your hard drive that's set up to emulate physical memory.

10.4 You can use Activity Monitor's System Memory tab to track how MacBook Air is using memory.

The pie chart shows how MacBook Air is currently allocating your computer's RAM. The total amount of RAM available appears below the pie chart. These four types of RAM appear:

- **Free.** This is the number of megabytes currently available for processes. As this number gets lower, system performance slows because MacBook Air may reduce the memory that each process uses. If this number (plus the Inactive number, described in this section) drops very low (a few megabytes), use the Activity Monitor to see if a process is using excessive amounts of memory.

- **Wired.** This is the number of megabytes that must stay in RAM and can't be stored on disk in virtual memory.

- **Active.** This is the number of megabytes currently stored in RAM and used by processes.

- **Inactive.** This is the number of megabytes currently stored in RAM and no longer used by processes. All this data has also been paged out to virtual memory, so the RAM is available for another process to use.

Besides these four types of RAM, the System Memory tab also displays five other values:

- **Used.** This is the total amount of information currently being stored in RAM. It's the sum of the Wired, Active, and Inactive values.

- **VM size.** This is the size, in gigabytes, of the virtual memory cache on the hard drive.

- **Page ins.** This is the amount of data that the system has read in from virtual memory. If this number grows quite large, it means MacBook Air's performance is not what it could be because the system must retrieve data from the relatively slow hard drive. You need to shut down some running programs or processes.

- **Page outs.** This is the amount of data that the system has had to write to the hard drive's virtual memory to free up real memory. This value is likely 0 most of the time, but it's okay if it's not. However, if it starts to get large (hundreds of megabytes) in a short time, it likely means that your system doesn't have enough real memory for the programs you're running.

- **Swap used.** This is the size of the swap file, which is the area of virtual memory that MacBook Air is actually using. So even though the entire virtual memory cache may be 25GB or 30GB, the swap file is (or should be) vastly smaller. It should actually be 0 most of the time, but it may grow to a few megabytes. If you see that it grows to hundreds of megabytes over a short period, MacBook Air likely doesn't have enough RAM for the programs you're running.

**Note** On any other Mac, you could solve most memory problems simply by adding more RAM to the system. Unfortunately, this isn't an option with MacBook Air because the memory chips are soldered to the motherboard, which means they can't be replaced or upgraded.

## Monitoring hard drive usage

Having enough RAM is crucial for system stability, but everything in RAM was originally stored on the hard drive. This means that it's nearly as important to monitor your hard drive activity. The crucial thing here is how often your system asks the hard drive to read data from, and write data to, the drive:

- **Reading data from the hard drive.** Hard drives are extremely fast and they read data from the drive all the time. However, a hard drive is still relatively slow compared to RAM, so if the hard drive has to read data excessively, it slows down your system. Excessive drive reading is most often a sign that your hard drive is fragmented.

● **Writing data to the hard drive.** If your hard drive is writing data back to the drive excessively, it's usually a sign that MacBook Air doesn't have enough RAM for all the programs that you're running. Try shutting down a few.

**Genius**

MacBook Air files don't easily get fragmented (that is, broken into smaller chunks and spread around the hard drive). This is probably why MacBook Air doesn't come with a disk-optimization utility to fix fragmentation. However, fragmenting can happen, so to fix it you need a program such as iDefrag from Coriolis Systems (www.coriolis-systems.com). It costs $29.95, but there's a demo version that defrags up to 100MB.

If you often get the spinning wait cursor (the rainbow-colored spinning cursor that appears when the system is taking its sweet time to complete some task), excessive drive reads and writes could be the culprit. To check, run Activity Monitor (in Finder, choose Applications ➪ Utilities ➪ Activity Monitor) and then click the Disk Activity tab, shown in Figure 10.5.

10.5 You can use Activity Monitor's Disk Activity tab to track how frequently the MacBook Air hard drive is reading and writing data.

**Note**

Spinning wait cursor is Apple's yawn-inducing name for the dreaded "busy" icon. Much more fun names for it are spinning pizza and, my favorite, spinning beach ball of death (SBOD).

There's a lot of data here, but you need to monitor only two values:

● **Reads in/sec.** This tells you the number of times per second the hard drive is reading data.

● **Writes out/sec.** This tells you the number of times per second the hard drive is writing data.

These values should be 0 most of the time, but they do jump up occasionally when you use MacBook Air. If you see these numbers jump up to any nonzero value and stay up for an extended period, you know that you have a problem.

# Checking for software updates

When Apple or a third-party software developer prepares an update to a program, new features, support for new technologies, performance boosts, and security enhancements are often included. However, the vast majority of items in a software update are fixes that squash bugs, provide more stability, and make the program more compatible with existing hardware.

In other words, if you're having consistent trouble with a program, chances are that other people have been having the same problem, the software developers know about the problem, and they've taken steps to fix it. This means that installing the most recent update for the application can be the cure you've been seeking.

You have two ways to check for software updates:

- **For Apple software.** Pull down the Apple menu and choose Software Update.

- **For other software developers.** Go to the company's website. First find your program's product page and check out the latest version number. If it's later than the version you have, see if you're eligible for a free (or at least cheap) upgrade. Otherwise, go to the site's support pages and look around to see if a patch or other update is available for your application.

**Genius**

To find out what version of a program you have, start the program and then choose *Program* ➪ About *Program* (where *Program* is the name of the application). The dialog that appears tells you the version number.

# Bypassing your login items

It's always possible that flaky system behavior could be caused by one of your login items. To find out, it's possible to log in without loading any of your login items (this is called a safe login). If the problem goes away, you're a step closer to locating the culprit.

First, follow these steps to log in without your login items:

1. **Pull down the Apple menu and choose Log Out** *User* **(where** *User* **is your username).** You can also press Shift+⌘+Q. MacBook Air asks if you're sure.

2. **Click Log Out.** MacBook Air logs you out and displays the login screen.

3. **Choose your user account (if necessary) and type your password.**

4. **Press and hold the Shift key and then click Log In.** MacBook Air logs you in without loading any of your login items.

5. **When you see the desktop, release the Shift key.**

If the problem goes away, you can be fairly certain that a login item is the cause. From here, disable the login items one at a time (as described in Chapter 7) until you find the one that's the source of your woes.

# Deleting a program's preferences file

A preferences file is a document that stores options and other data that you've entered using the application's Preferences command. One of the most common causes of application flakiness is a preferences file that's somehow become damaged or corrupted (for example, its data is written with the wrong syntax). In that case, you can solve the problem by deleting (or moving) the preferences file so that the application has to rebuild it. On the downside, this may mean that you have to reenter some preferences, but that's usually a fairly small price to pay for a stable application.

Preferences files use the PLIST filename extension. In most cases, the filename uses the following general format: com.*company.application*.plist.

Here, *company* is the name of the software company that makes the application, and *application* is the name of the program. Here are some examples:

com.apple.iTunes.plist

com.microsoft.Word.plist

com.adobe.PhotoshopElements.plist

Follow these steps to delete an application's preferences file.

1. **Quit the application if it's currently running.**

2. **In Finder, hold down the Option key and then choose Go ⇨ Library.** Mac OS X opens the Library folder.

3. **Double-click Preferences.** Mac OS X opens the Preferences folder.

4. **Locate the application's preferences file.** If you can't find the preferences file, choose Macintosh HD ⇨ Library ⇨ Preferences and see if it appears in that folder.

5. **Click and drag the preferences file, and drop it in another location.** The desktop is probably the best spot for this. Note that if the application has multiple preferences files, you should move all of them to the new location.

**Note** Unfortunately, not every preferences file uses the com.*company.application*.plist format. If you can't find the preferences file you're looking for, type either the company name or the program name in the Search box.

6. **Run the application and see if the problem persists.**

   - **Problem resolved.** The preferences file was the source after all, so go ahead and move it to the Trash from the location you chose in Step 5. You need to reenter your preferences.

   - **Problem remains.** The preferences file wasn't the culprit after all. Quit the application and move the preferences file back to the Preferences folder from the location you chose in Step 5.

## Reinstalling Mac OS X

If worse comes to worst and MacBook Air won't start, or if it's just completely unstable, you need to bite the bullet and reinstall the operating system. If you still have access to the system, it's a good idea to make backups of your documents, just in case something goes wrong during the transfer. Chapter 7 addresses various ways to back up your files.

With that done, launch the Install Mac OS X application:

- **Mac OS X Lion.** Boot to the Recovery HD, as described later in this chapter. When you see the Mac OS X Utilities application, click Reinstall Mac OS X and then click Continue.

**Note** If you had to replace your MacBook Air hard drive, the Recovery HD won't be available to you. In that case, you can purchase a Mac OS X Lion Install USB thumb drive from Apple for the rather steep price of $69.

- **Previous version of Mac OS X.** Insert the Mac OS X Install DVD or USB flash drive, turn on or restart your Mac, and hold down C while your Mac is restarting. You can release C when you see the Apple logo. Your Mac boots to the Mac OS X Install DVD or flash drive.

# General Hardware Troubleshooting Techniques

If you're having trouble with a device attached to MacBook Air, the good news is that a fair chunk of hardware problems have a relatively limited set of causes. You may be able to get the device back on its feet by attempting a few tried-and-true remedies that work quite often for many devices. The next few sections take you through these generic troubleshooting techniques.

# Basic hardware troubleshooting steps

If it's not immediately obvious what the problem is, your MacBook Air hardware troubleshooting routine should always start with these very basic techniques:

- **Check connections, power switches, and so on.** Some of the most common (and most embarrassing) causes of hardware problems are the simple physical things, such as devices being unplugged or disconnected. So your first troubleshooting steps should concentrate on the obvious: making sure that a device is turned on, checking that cable connections are secure, and ensuring that external devices (such as those using a Thunderbolt or USB cable) are properly connected.

  For example, if you can't access the Internet or your network, make sure that your network's router or wireless access point is turned on. If you have a wired connection, make sure that the network cable between MacBook Air and your router is properly connected.

- **Replace the batteries.** Wireless devices, such as keyboards and mice, really chew through batteries. If either one is working intermittently or not at all, always try replacing the batteries to see if that solves the problem.

- **Turn the device off and then on.** You power cycle a device by turning it off, waiting a few seconds for its innards to stop spinning, and then turning it back on. You'd be amazed how often this simple procedure can get a device back up and running. Of course, not all devices have an on/off switch, but this technique works very well for devices such as external displays, printers, scanners, routers, switches, modems, external hard drives and DVD drives; many Thunderbolt, USB, and FireWire devices; and some wireless devices, such as mice and keyboards.

  Many wireless mice have a reset button on the bottom, whereas some keyboards — notably the Apple Bluetooth keyboard — have an on/off switch. Thunderbolt, USB, and FireWire devices often get their power directly from the corresponding port. Power cycle these devices by unplugging them and then plugging them back in.

**Genius**

If you're getting a network error or you can't access the Internet, the router may be at fault. Power off the router and then power it on again. Wait until the status lights stabilize and then try accessing the network. If you still can't access the Internet, try the same thing with your modem.

- **Close all programs.** If you have lots of programs going, device drivers (the little programs that enable Mac OS X to communicate with devices, and vice versa) may get weird because there isn't enough memory or other resources. You can often fix flaky behavior by shutting down all your open programs and starting again.

- **Log out.** Logging off serves to clear the memory by shutting down your programs, but it also releases much of the stuff MacBook Air has loaded into memory, thus creating a slightly cleaner palette than just closing your programs. To log out, pull down the Apple menu and choose Log Out *User* (where *User* is the MacBook Air username), or just press Shift +⌘+Q.

- **Reset the device's default settings.** If you can configure a device, perhaps some new setting is causing the problem. If you recently made a change, try returning the setting to its original value. If that doesn't do the trick, most configurable devices have some kind of Restore Default Settings option that enables you to quickly return the device to its factory settings.

- **Upgrade the device's firmware.** Some devices come with *firmware*, a small program that runs inside the device and controls its internal functions. For example, all routers have firmware. Check with the manufacturer to see if a new version exists. If it does, download the new version and then see the device's manual to learn how to upgrade the firmware.

Firmware updates for the MacBook Air can be particularly tricky. Be sure to follow the instructions and do not interrupt the restart sequence. When restarting your network, remember to follow this sequence: Reboot the digital modem, reboot the wired or wireless router, and then restart your MacBook Air.

# Restarting MacBook Air

If a hardware device is having a problem with some system files, logging off MacBook Air won't help because the system files remain loaded. By rebooting MacBook Air, you reload the entire system, which is often enough to solve many computer problems. You reboot MacBook Air by pulling down the Apple menu, choosing Restart, and then clicking Restart in the dialog that appears.

## Power cycling MacBook Air

For problem devices that don't have a power switch — basically, anything inside MacBook Air, including the display — restarting MacBook Air might not resolve the problem because the devices remain powered up the whole time. You can power cycle these devices as a group by power cycling MacBook Air:

1. **Close all running applications.**

2. **Pull down the Apple menu and choose Shut Down.** MacBook Air asks you to confirm.

3. **Click Shut Down.** MacBook Air shuts down the system.

4. **Once MacBook Air shuts off, wait for 30 seconds to give all devices time to spin down.**

5. **Turn MacBook Air back on.**

## Forcing a stuck MacBook Air to restart or shut down

If things go seriously awry on MacBook Air, you may find that you can't do anything and your applications are frozen. You can bang away at the keyboard all you want but nothing happens. The mouse pointer doesn't even budge when you move the mouse. That's a major-league lockup you have there, and your only recourse is to force MacBook Air to restart or shut down.

- **Forcing MacBook Air to restart.** Press and hold the Control and ⌘ keys, and then press the power button.

- **Forcing MacBook Air to shut down.** Press and hold the power button until MacBook Air shuts off.

**Caution**

Forcing MacBook Air to restart or shut down doesn't give you any graceful way to close your running applications. This means that if you have unsaved changes in any open documents, you lose them. Therefore, it's a good idea to make sure MacBook Air is frozen and not just in a temporary state of suspended animation while it's waiting for some lengthy process to finish. If you're not sure, wait 5 minutes before forcing the restart or shutdown.

## Restarting MacBook Air in Safe Mode

Login items — programs that run automatically when you log in to MacBook Air — can cause system problems by using up resources and creating memory conflicts. However, they're not the only behind-the-scenes components that can make your system wonky. Other processes that MacBook Air and your applications use can run amok and cause trouble.

To see whether such a process is at the root of your problem, you can perform a Safe Boot. That is, you can start MacBook Air in Safe Mode, which means that it doesn't load most of those behind-the-scenes components. If the problem still persists in Safe Mode, you know it's not caused by a hidden process. If the problem does go away, it's a bit harder to deal with because there's no way to disable individual components. You may need to reinstall Mac OS X, as described earlier.

Follow these steps to perform a Safe Boot:

1. **Pull down the Apple menu and choose Shut Down.** MacBook Air asks if you're sure.

2. **Click Shut Down.** MacBook Air logs you out and then shuts off.

3. **Press the power button to turn MacBook Air back on.**

4. **Press and hold the Shift key until you see the Apple logo.** MacBook Air loads with only a minimal set of components. When you get to the login screen, you see the words Safe Boot.

**Note**

Although you might think it would take MacBook Air less time to load without all those extra components, the opposite is actually the case. MacBook Air takes quite a bit longer to start up in Safe Mode. If you want to know why, see the following page: http://support.apple.com/kb/HT1564.

5. **Log in to MacBook Air.** Check to see if the problem is still present. If it is, continue with the troubleshooting techniques in the following sections.

## Restarting MacBook Air using the Recovery HD

You can recover from some problems by accessing the recovery tools that are available if your MacBook Air is running Mac OS X Lion. All Macs that have Mac OS X Lion installed have a hidden area of the hard drive called Recovery HD, which contains a program called Mac OS X Utilities. This program offers various tools that you can use to troubleshoot and recover from problems. For example, if you suspect that your Mac's main hard drive is causing a problem, you can access Recovery HD and use a tool called Disk Utility to repair the drive. Similarly, you can also use Recovery HD to restore your Mac from a Time Machine backup, and to reinstall Mac OS X Lion.

**Note**

If the entire MacBook Air hard drive is toast, you won't be able to access the Recovery HD. Here's hoping you read Chapter 7 and so have the Mac OS X Lion Recovery tools on a flash drive or external hard drive.

To access the Mac OS X Recovery drive, restart your MacBook Air while holding down the Option key. After a few seconds, your MacBook Air displays a list of the available start-up drives, as shown in Figure 10.6.

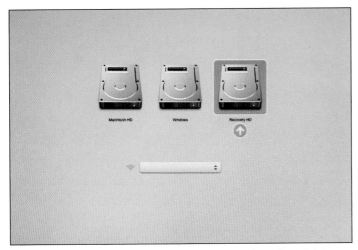

10.6 Hold down the Option key as you restart MacBook Air, then click Recovery HD.

Click the Recovery HD icon, and a few seconds later the Mac OS X Utilities application appears, as shown in Figure 10.7.

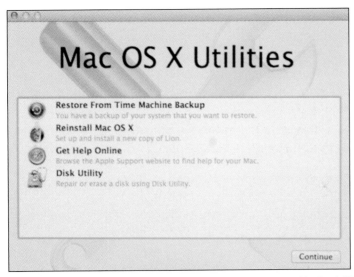

10.7 Use Mac OS X Lion's Recovery tools to repair or restore your MacBook Air.

**Genius**

If you can't start MacBook Air, you can still access troubleshooting information on the web. Boot to the Recovery HD, click the Wi-Fi Status icon, click your Wi-Fi network, and then type your Wi-Fi password, if prompted. In the Mac OS X Utilities window, click Get Help Online and then click Continue. Mac OS X Utilities loads Safari and displays some troubleshooting steps. However, you can also use Safari to surf to any site that has the information you seek.

## Restarting MacBook Air using the Mac OS X Install USB flash drive

If you can't access the Recovery HD and you don't have an external Recovery flash drive or external hard drive, then you need to order the Mac OS X Lion Install USB flash drive from Apple. It's expensive ($69!), but it just might be worth it if it helps get MacBook Air back on its feet.

Once you have the drive, follow these steps to boot MacBook Air:

1. **Insert the Mac OS X Install USB flash drive into MacBook Air.**

2. **Restart MacBook Air.**

3. **During the restart, press and hold C.** When you see the Apple icon, you can release C. MacBook Air boots to the USB flash drive.

## Restarting MacBook Air in target disk mode

If you can't boot MacBook Air, you can't access the Recovery HD, and you don't have either a Recovery disk or the Mac OS X Install flash drive, you might think you're out of luck. Not yet! If you have access to a second Mac that supports Thunderbolt, your last option is to restart MacBook Air in target disk mode. Here's how:

1. **Connect MacBook Air and the other Mac using a Thunderbolt cable.**

2. **Restart MacBook Air.**

3. **During the restart, hold down T until you see the Thunderbolt icon.** MacBook Air is now in target disk mode.

4. **Restart the other Mac.**

5. **When the other Mac's desktop appears, the MacBook Air's hard drive appears as a drive on the other Mac.** This enables you to use Disk Utility on the other Mac to verify or repair the MacBook Air hard drive.

# Repairing the hard drive

If MacBook Air won't start, or if an application freezes, it's possible that an error on the hard drive is causing the problem. To see if this is the case, you need to repair the hard drive using MacBook Air's Disk Utility program. How are you supposed to do that if you can't even start MacBook Air? Good question! The answer is that you need to restart MacBook Air using a secondary boot device: the Recovery HD, an external Recovery disk, the Mac OS X Install flash drive, or in target disk mode using another Mac (see the previous three sections for the details). You then run Disk Utility from the secondary boot device, which enables you to repair your main hard drive. Note, too, that even if you can start MacBook Air, you still need to boot to the secondary device because you can't repair the main hard drive while it's being used by MacBook Air.

**Caution**

Because repairing your hard drive can occasionally cause problems, be sure to back it up before attempting the repair (assuming you can access Mac OS X).

Follow these steps to repair your hard drive:

1. **Restart MacBook Air using a secondary boot device.**

2. **Launch Disk Utility.** Use one of the following procedures, depending on which device you boot to:

   ● **Mac OS X Lion Recovery HD partition.** Click Disk Utility and then click Continue.

   ● **Mac in target disk mode.** Open Finder on the other Mac and choose Applications ⇨ Utilities ⇨ Disk Utility.

   ● **Mac OS X Install flash drive.** When you get to the Mac OS X Installer screen, choose Utilities ⇨ Disk Utility.

3. **Choose Macintosh HD, which is the hard drive you want to repair.** If MacBook Air is in target disk mode, be sure to click the Macintosh HD that appears under the AAPL Thunderbolt Target Media disk.

4. **Make sure the First Aid tab is selected, as shown in Figure 10.8.**

5. **Click Repair Disk.** Disk Utility verifies that the drive is sound and fixes any problems that it finds.

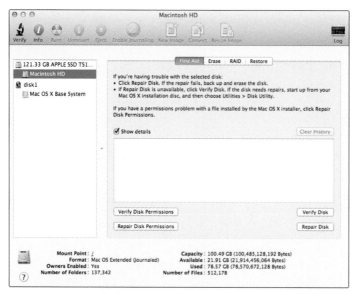

10.8 You can repair the hard drive on your MacBook Air by running Disk
Utility from a secondary boot device.

**Genius**

Ideally, Disk Utility reports that "The volume Macintosh HD appears to be OK." In the
worst-case scenario, Disk Utility reports that it found errors, but it can't fix them. In
that case, you need to turn to a more heavy-duty solution, such as a third-party disk
repair application. I recommend these two: DiskWarrior (www.alsoft.com) and
TechTool Pro (www.micromat.com).

# Repairing disk permissions

All the files on MacBook Air have permissions applied to them. *Permissions* are a collection of settings that determine what users, or groups of users, can do with each file. For example, if a file
implements read-only permissions, it means that all users can only read the contents of the file —
they can't make any changes to it or delete it.

For things such as system files, particular permissions are set during installation and shouldn't ever
be changed. If a system file's permissions do happen to change, it can cause all kinds of problems,
including program lockups and flaky system behavior.

Fortunately, Disk Utility has a feature that enables you to repair permissions for many of the files on your system. Here's how it works:

1. **If you can't start MacBook Air, boot using a secondary device.** Otherwise, boot MacBook Air normally.

2. **Launch Disk Utility.** Use one of the following procedures based on your boot method:

   - **MacBook Air.** Choose Applications ⇨ Utilities ⇨ Disk Utility.

   - **Mac OS X Lion Recovery HD partition.** Click Disk Utility and then click Continue.

   - **Mac in target disk mode.** Open Finder on the other Mac and choose Applications ⇨ Utilities ⇨ Disk Utility.

   - **Mac OS X Install flash drive.** When you get to the Mac OS X Installer screen, choose Utilities ⇨ Disk Utility.

   - **Mac OS X Install DVD.** When you get to the Mac OS X Installer screen, choose Utilities ⇨ Disk Utility.

3. **Choose Macintosh HD, which is the hard drive with the permissions you want to repair.**

4. **Make sure the First Aid tab is selected.**

5. **Click Repair Disk Permissions.** Disk Utility repairs the permissions.

# How Do I Solve Specific Software Problems?

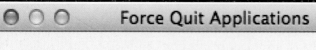

### Force Quit Applications

If an application doesn't respond for a while, select its name and click Force Quit.

 iTunes (not responding)

 Safari

System Preferences

 Finder

You can open this window by pressing Command–Option–Escape.

**Force Quit**

You saw quite a few general solutions to software woes in Chapter 10, and those remedies should stand you in good stead for many of the problems that come your way. Unfortunately, those "big picture" fixes don't always work because quite often a problem requires a more specific set of steps to solve what's ailing your Mac. To that end, this chapter takes you through quite a few such specific solutions to some of the most common Mac software glitches.

# You Can't Change Some Options in System Preferences

When you open System Preferences and click an icon, you may find that some or all of the controls in the resulting preferences window are disabled. This actually isn't a glitch or a bug at all. Instead, it's a security feature designed to prevent unauthorized users from making changes to sensitive system settings. (It's also designed to prevent you from making certain changes without at least having to think about them first.) For example, Figure 11.1 shows what the Parental Controls preferences look like when a user without authorization displays the window.

11.1 MacBook Air sometimes locks preferences to avoid unauthorized changes.

To enable the controls, click the lock icon in the bottom-left corner of the window and then, if prompted, type the username and password of an administrator account.

# A Program Is Stuck

When you're working away on your MacBook Air, you may suddenly find that it's unresponsive and you're faced with the dreaded spinning wait cursor that just won't stop or go away.

It's possible that your program is stuck, but that's not guaranteed.

- **The program could just be really busy.** Sometimes program operations take an inordinately long time. Recalculating a large spreadsheet, compiling a program, or rendering a 3-D object can take minutes. Therefore, your first resort should be to wait for a while to see if the program works itself out of its trance.

- **Your Mac may be low on memory.** This can cause a program to seem stuck, when in fact it's really just trying to struggle through on limited resources. Try shutting down some of your other programs to free up some RAM.

If none of this works, you have no choice but to force the program to quit. Here are the steps to follow:

11.2 Use the Force Quit Applications window to shut down a misbehaving application.

1. **Pull down the Apple menu and choose Force Quit.** You can also press Option+⌘+Esc. You see the Force Quit Applications window shown in Figure 11.2.

2. **Click the recalcitrant application.**

3. **Click Force Quit.** Your MacBook Air asks if you're sure you want to do this.

4. **Click Force Quit.**

**Note**

If the stubborn application still won't quit, try running the Force Quit command again. The second time is often the charm when forcing rogue applications to shut down. No go? Okay, now try quitting the application's process, as described in the next section. If the program remains running, shut down the rest of your applications and then restart your Mac.

# A Process Is Stuck

What happens if the Dock locks up or a Spotlight search hangs? In these cases, if you try the Force Quit command you're out of luck because processes, such as the Dock and Spotlight, don't show up in the Force Quit Applications window.

However, they do show up in the Activity Monitor. You can use Activity Monitor to force these and any other stuck processes to quit. Here are the steps to follow:

1. **Click Finder in the Dock.**

2. **Choose Applications ⇨ Utilities ⇨ Activity Monitor.** The Activity Monitor window appears.

3. **Choose the process that you want to quit, as shown in Figure 11.3.**

11.3 To quit a process, choose it in Activity Monitor and then click Quit Process.

4. **Click Quit Process.** Activity Monitor asks you to confirm.

5. **Click Force Quit.**

**Caution**

Processes used by the system itself usually appear as Root in the User column of the Activity Monitor. These processes are critical to the functioning of your Mac, so don't quit any of them or you might lock up your machine.

# Solving Program Problems

Almost everything you do on MacBook Air requires a program, so you can't do much if one refuses to run, either because it crashes or refuses to open in the first place. The next couple of sections offer some solutions to these program woes.

# A program crashes

One of the more frustrating Mac experiences is to be merrily working away in an application when, out of the blue, the program simply disappears from the screen. Apple says that the application "quit unexpectedly," but the rest of us call this a good old-fashioned program crash.

When an application crashes, you usually see a dialog like the one shown in Figure 11.4. Click Relaunch to get MacBook Air to restart the application for you. In most cases, the program picks itself up, dusts itself off, and resumes working as though nothing bad had happened.

11.4 This dialog appears when an application goes up in flames.

However, you may find that the program goes down for the count yet again. In this case, you see the dialog shown in Figure 11.5. Click Reset and relaunch.

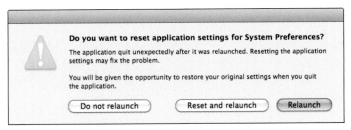

11.5 This dialog appears when an application crashes a second time.

At this point in the proceedings, MacBook Air assumes that a corrupt preferences file is causing the problem. So when you click Reset and relaunch, MacBook Air does three things:

- **It creates a copy of the application's existing preferences file.** This copy has the same name as the original, with .saved tacked onto the end.
- **It deletes the application's existing preferences file.**
- **It restarts the application.** The application sees that a new preferences file exists, so it creates a new default preferences file.

This procedure is called *Safe Relaunch*. If your application runs without mishap now, the preferences file was the troublemaker all along. Go ahead and type your preferences again. When you exit the application, MacBook Air displays the dialog shown in Figure 11.6. Be sure to click Use new settings to save your new preferences file.

213

If the preferences file isn't the problem (that is, the application keeps crashing even after a Safe Relaunch), use the following trouble-shooting steps, in this order:

1. **Restart MacBook Air.**

2. **Install an update for the software if one is available.**

11.6 This dialog appears when you shut down an application that started earlier with Safe Relaunch.

3. **If it's a third-party application, reinstall the application.**

**Genius**

Before you get too involved in troubleshooting a program crash, consider a simpler explanation. Does the crash always occur when you're working with a particular file? If so, there's an excellent chance that the problem lies not with the application, but with the file. If the file contains important data, and you can work with it for a time before the crash occurs, copy the data and paste it into a new file. Then trash the old file.

## A program won't start

Occasionally you'll try to start a program and nothing happens. If you clicked a Dock icon to launch the application, all you see is the icon endlessly (and, eventually, maddeningly) bouncing up and down. This happened to me once when I tried to launch iWeb on a brand new iMac!

If this happens, try the following fixes, in this order:

1. **Restart MacBook Air.**

2. **Install an update for the software if one is available.** (This solved my iWeb problem.)

3. **Delete the application's preferences file.** This process is explained in Chapter 10.

4. **If it's a third-party application, reinstall it.**

# You Can't Empty the Trash

When you attempt to empty the Trash, you may receive an error message, such as the one shown in Figure 11.7. To solve this problem,

11.7 You might see this dialog when you try to empty the Trash.

either click Remove All Items in the dialog, or press and hold the Option key while you choose the Empty Trash command.

MacBook Air may also tell you that you don't have permission to delete a file. In this case, you need to follow these steps to solve the problem:

1. **In Finder, choose Applications ⇨ Utilities ⇨ Terminal.** The Terminal window opens.

2. **Type** cd ~/.Trash **and press Return.**

3. **Type** sudo rm –rf **and then add a space at the end of the command, but don't press Return just yet.**

4. **Right-click the Trash icon and then click Open.**

5. **Choose Edit ⇨ Select All.** You can also press ⌘+A.

6. **Click and drag the selected Trash files and drop them inside the Terminal window.**

7. **Return to the Terminal window and press Return.** Terminal prompts you for an administrator password.

8. **Type your password (it doesn't appear on-screen) and then press Return.** Terminal deletes all the files from the Trash.

# You Can't Run Administrator Commands in Terminal

Certain Mac operations require you to open the Terminal application and run a command as an administrator by using the sudo (super user do) command. When you first enter the sudo (pronounced soo-doo) command followed by the actual command you want to execute, Terminal prompts you for your MacBook Air administrator password.

It's important to note that the sudo command requires some kind of password. If your MacBook Air administrator password is blank, you might be tempted to press Return when sudo asks you for a password. Unfortunately, that won't work because sudo will simply drop you back off at the command prompt without doing anything.

If you want to run administrator commands in Terminal, you must create a nonblank password for your MacBook Air administrator account. This has the added benefit of greatly increasing your MacBook Air security because the administrator account should always have a nonblank password.

# You Can't Send Email

When you compose messages using Apple Mail on MacBook Air, you may find that you can't send those messages. For example, the Send button may be disabled, or you may receive bounce messages from your ISP telling you that the messages could not be delivered.

A disabled Send button almost always means that you haven't selected or configured an outgoing mail server for your account. If you know you already have an outgoing mail server (also called an SMTP — Simple Mail Transport Protocol — server) configured, follow these steps to select it:

1. **In Mail, select Mail ⇨ Preferences.** The Mail preferences appear.
2. **Click Accounts.** Mail displays a list of your email accounts.
3. **In the Accounts lists, choose the one with which you want to work.**
4. **Click the Account Information pane.**
5. **In the Outgoing Mail Server (SMTP) pop-up menu, choose the server you want to use for sending your messages, as shown in Figure 11.8.** Mail now enables the Send button and uses this server to send your messages.

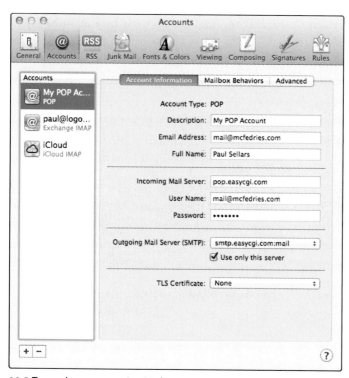

11.8 To send messages using Mail, you must choose an SMTP server.

If you see only None in the Outgoing Mail Server (SMTP) menu, you need to configure an SMTP server to use with your account. From the Account Information pane, use the Outgoing Mail Server (SMTP) pop-up menu to choose Edit SMTP Server List. Click + to create a new server entry and then enter the server details.

If you already had an SMTP server selected, the likely reason that you can't send email is that the server isn't configured correctly. From the Account Information pane, use the Outgoing Mail Server (SMTP) pop-up menu to choose Edit SMTP Server List, and then choose your SMTP server.

Check the following three things:

- **Using the Server Name text box, make sure the address of the SMTP server is the same as the address provided to you by your ISP or mail host.** Note that almost all SMTP servers have an address in the form of: mail.*provider*.com or smtp.*provider*.com (where *provider* is the domain name of the ISP or host).

- **In the Advanced pane (see Figure 11.9), make sure the port value is the same as the port number provided to you by your ISP or mail host.** In most cases the port number should be 25, particularly if this is your ISP's SMTP server. However, third-party mail hosts may need to use a port other than 25 because many ISPs block outgoing messages over port 25 if the sending account isn't associated with the ISP. For example, suppose you have an account with an ISP and another with iCloud. If you try to send a message from your iCloud account over port 25, chances are your ISP will block it (and return an error message).

  To fix this problem, you need to contact the third-party host to see if it offers an alternative SMTP port (such as port 587, which is supported by iCloud). If the alternative port is either 465 or 587, be sure to select the Use default ports (25, 465, 587) option, as shown in Figure 11.9. Otherwise, select the Use custom port option, and then type the port number in the text box.

**Note**

Why do most ISPs not allow third-party accounts to use port 25 nowadays? It's primarily a security issue, because most spammers try to hide their tracks by "relaying" their messages through ISP mail servers. Allowing only ISP accounts to use the ISP's mail server prevents this.

- **In the Advanced tab, check the Authentication value.** If your ISP or mail host requires authentication before it allows a message to be sent, you must choose the correct type of security from this list. Most providers require Password security, so also double-check that the values in the User Name and Password fields are correct. (In most cases, you use the same login data that you use to check for incoming mail.)

**11.9** To troubleshoot mail-sending problems, use the Advanced pane to check the server port and authentication.

# Repairing Remote Disc Woes

MacBook Air doesn't come with a built-in optical (CD or DVD) drive. However, as explained in Chapter 2, that's not necessarily a huge deal because you can use the Remote Disc application to connect to a CD or DVD drive on another Mac. However, Remote Disc doesn't always work as advertised, so the next few sections take you through a few troubleshooting steps.

# Remote Disc won't connect to certain CDs or DVDs

When you attempt to connect to a remote optical drive, you may receive an error message similar to the one shown in Figure 11.10.

This error message isn't actually an error at all.

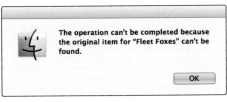

**11.10** MacBook Air's Remote Disc application may display an error similar to the one shown here when connecting with certain discs.

Instead, it's a copyright protection feature. That is, Remote Disc won't connect to an audio CD, a movie DVD, or any other disc that has built-in copyright features. The only solution is to play the disc directly on MacBook Air using an external drive, such as the MacBook Air SuperDrive.

# Remote Disc can't see the host computer

When you're using the Remote Disc application, the host computer is the remote Mac that's sharing its DVD drive. When you open Finder and click Remote Disc, you should see the host computer icon. If you don't see it, the likely reason is that the host computer's firewall is blocking Remote Disc connections. A *firewall* is a security feature that monitors a computer's incoming connections to ensure that no unauthorized data makes it through.

Follow these steps on the host computer to ensure that it accepts Remote Disc connections:

1. **Click System Preferences in the Dock.** The System Preferences window opens.

2. **Click Security & Privacy.** The Security & Privacy preferences appear.

3. **Click the Firewall pane.**

4. **If the firewall is currently turned on, click the lock icon and then type your MacBook Air administrator username and password.** If, instead, the firewall is currently turned off, you can skip the rest of these steps because MacBook Air automatically allows Remote Disc connections when the firewall is off.

5. **Click Advanced to display the firewall advanced settings.**

6. **Make sure the Block all incoming connections option is deselected, as shown in Figure 11.11.**

7. **Click OK.**

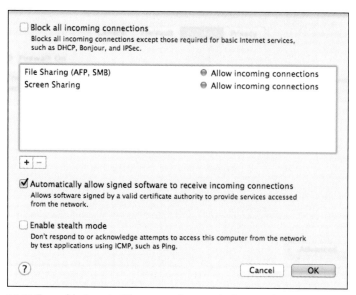

**11.11** To enable Remote Disc connections on the host, make sure the firewall is not blocking incoming connections.

# You can't use Remote Disc with a Windows drive

Remote Disc works best with another Mac as the host computer because Macs have the DVD or CD Sharing feature built in (assuming it's running at least Mac OS X 10.4.10). If you don't have a Mac that comes with DVD or CD Sharing, or if MacBook Air is your only Mac, you might want to use a Windows computer on your network as the host computer. However, that's a problem because Windows doesn't come with the DVD or CD Sharing feature. Fortunately, you can work around this problem by installing that feature on the Windows PC you want to use as the host.

To use Remote Disc with Windows, the Windows PC must be running Windows 7, Windows Vista, or Windows XP with Service Pack 2 or later. Follow these steps:

1. **On the Windows PC, use a web browser to navigate to** http://support.apple.com/kb/ DL112. If you're running Windows 7, don't sweat that (at least, as I write this) the system requirements only mention Windows Vista and XP. DVD or CD Sharing works fine in Windows 7.

2. **Click Download to download the DVD or CD Sharing Installer, and then run the program.** The DVD or CD Sharing Installer appears, as shown in Figure 11.12.

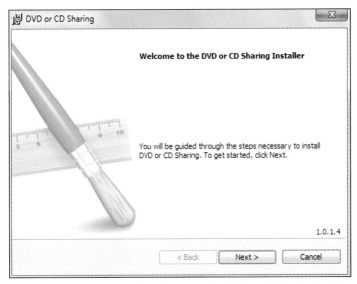

**11.12** In Windows, download and then run the DVD or CD Sharing Installer.

3. **Click Next.** The DVD or CD Sharing Installer shows you which folder it will use for the installation.

4. **Click Install and then type your User Account Control credentials, if prompted.** The Installer sets up DVD or CD Sharing on the Windows PC.

5. **Click Finish.**

6. **Choose Start ⇨ Control Panel.** The Control Panel window appears.

7. **Display all the Control Panel icons.**

   - **Windows 7.** In the View By list, choose either Small icons or Large icons.

   - **Windows Vista.** Click Classic View.

   - **Windows XP.** Click Switch to Classic View.

8. **Double-click the DVD or CD Sharing Options icon.** The DVD or CD Sharing dialog appears.

**Caution** When you use a Mac as the Remote Disk host machine, pressing the Eject button on the host opens a dialog that warns you the disc is being used by another computer, which is a great feature. Unfortunately, the Windows version of DVD or CD Sharing doesn't come with this feature. This means that if the Windows user tries to eject the disc, no warning appears, the disc ejects, and MacBook Air loses access to the disc.

9. **Select the Enable DVD or CD Sharing check box, as shown in Figure 11.13.**

10. **If you want the operator of the Windows PC to be able to approve the remote use of the DVD drive (this is always a good idea), leave the Ask me before allowing others to use my DVD drive check box selected.**

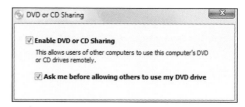

11.13 On the Windows PC, select the Enable DVD or CD Sharing check box.

11. **Click the X to close the box.**

You can now use Remote Disc on MacBook Air to access the DVD drive on the Windows PC. The technique is the same as it is with a host Mac.

**Note**

The next time you start Windows, you might see the Windows Security dialog telling you that Windows Firewall is blocking the DVD or CD Sharing program. Click Unblock to tell Windows Firewall to let the program do its thing. (To make this happen in Vista, you'll need to type your User Account Control credentials.)

# Time Machine No Longer Backs Up to an External Hard Drive

Time Machine is a real lifesaver when you need to recover a file or folder, but only if it consistently backs up MacBook Air. If Time Machine works for a while, but you then start getting errors and Time Machine reports that it can no longer back up to your external hard drive, what could be the problem?

The most likely culprit is that Time Machine has backed up 10GB of data to the drive, but that drive is configured in such a way that it can't store more than 10GB. Specifically, it means the drive is configured with the Master Boot Record partition type. To store more than 10GB on that hard drive, you must change the partition type to one that supports more data. Follow these steps:

1. **In Finder, press Shift+⌘+U to open the Utilities folder.**

2. **Double-click Disk Utility.** The Disk Utility window appears.

3. **Click the external hard drive.**

4. **Click the Partition pane.**

5. **In the Volume Scheme menu, choose 1 Partition.**

6. **In the Name text box, type a name for the partition.** The standard name is External HD, but you can use something more descriptive, such as Time Machine Backups.

7. **Click Options.** Disk Utility displays the partition scheme options.

8. **Select the GUID Partition Table option, as shown in Figure 11.14.**

Choose a partition scheme appropriate for the way you will use this disk:

⦿ GUID Partition Table

To use the disk to start up an Intel-based Mac, or to use the disk as a non-startup disk with any Mac with Mac OS X version 10.4 or later.

○ Apple Partition Map

To use the disk to start up a PowerPC-based Mac, or to use the disk as a non-startup disk with any Mac.

○ Master Boot Record

To use the disk to start up DOS and Windows computers, or to use with devices that require a DOS-compatible or Windows-compatible partition.

Default          Cancel          OK

11.14 For Time Machine backups to store data beyond 10GB, select the GUID Partition Table option.

9. **Click OK.**

10. **Click Apply.** Disk Utility warns you that all the data on the hard drive will be erased and asks you to confirm.

11. **Click Partition.** Disk Utility partitions the external hard drive.

12. **When the partition is complete, choose Disk Utility ⇨ Quit Disk Utility.**

13. **Open System Preferences.**

14. **Click the Time Machine icon.**

15. **Click Select Disk.**

16. **Click your external hard drive and then click Use Backup Disk.** MacBook Air is now configured to use the repartitioned drive for Time Machine backups.

# Solving Safari Troubles

Safari runs smoothly for the most part, but sometimes you'll need to overcome obstacles or simply adjust some preferences, such as how Safari tracks your web browsing. On rare occasions, you may encounter a website that won't open. You can work around that with Terminal. Even exporting your old Favorites from Internet Explorer isn't an insurmountable task for Safari!

## You want to hide your browsing tracks in Safari

The sites you visit on your own time are nobody else's business but your own, of course. However, in the interest of convenience, Safari keeps careful track of the sites you visit and the pages within those sites that you load. This information is stored in various Safari areas, particularly the history, but also in cookies and the Downloads window. If you're worried about other people seeing where you've been browsing, you need to remove some (or all) of this data.

For starters, consider the fact that it's distressingly easy to take a wrong turn on the web and end up in a bad part of town. You might click an apparently innocuous link in a web page or an email message, and land on a page that contains pornography, spam links, phishing code, or even malware. Of course you make tracks to a safer neighborhood right away, but that site still lurks in your browser history. To ensure that no one sees the site in your history and to prevent you (or someone else) from accidentally revisiting the site, you should delete it from the history.

Follow these steps:

1. **In Safari, choose History ⇨ Show All History to display the history list.** You can also click the Show All Bookmarks icon on the left side of the Bookmarks Bar and then click History in the Collections pane.
2. **Right-click the page you want to remove.**
3. **Click Delete**. Safari removes the page from the history.

If you don't want any sites or pages to appear in your history, you can clear out the whole thing by choosing History ⇨ Clear History.

Clearing the browser history is all well and good, but you're just fooling yourself if you think that your browsing activities are now safe from prying eyes. Even a moderately skilled snoop could still find out all about where you've been by checking your cookies, the Downloads window, Google search entries, and, most importantly, the browser's cache of saved site files. You're a wide-open book, my friend.

If you want to close that book, you need to take things a step further and clear everything. Safari calls this resetting the program and you do it with just a few steps:

1. **Choose Safari ⇨ Reset Safari.** The Reset Safari dialog appears, as shown in Figure 11.15.

2. **Select the options that you do not want Safari to reset.** For maximum privacy, you should select all of the options. However, you might want to deselect the Close all Safari windows option if you plan to continue using the program.

3. **Click Reset.** Safari resets the items you selected.

11.15 Use the Reset Safari dialog to erase all of your browsing tracks.

If you find yourself constantly resetting Safari, you can save yourself a bit of time by configuring Safari to reset itself automatically. This is called *private browsing* and it means that Safari doesn't save any data as you browse:

- Sites aren't added to the history (although the Back and Forward buttons still work for navigating sites that you've visited in the current session).

- Files aren't added to the Downloads window.

- Searched text isn't saved with the Google search box.

- AutoFill text isn't saved.

To activate private browsing, choose Safari ⇨ Private Browsing and click OK when Safari asks if you're sure you want to turn on private browsing. Safari activates the private browsing feature. That's how easy it is.

## A website doesn't recognize Safari

Some primitive or poorly coded websites may not show up properly because they don't recognize Safari. In some extreme cases, the site might not let you in at all if Safari isn't a supported browser (see Figure 11.16).

11.16 Some annoying websites don't support Safari and you can't visit them.

There's not much you can do directly to combat this browser discrimination, but you can fight back indirectly. The site is probably deciding which browsers are legitimate by using code to examine a string called the *user agent*. All browsers provide this string as a kind of identification. You can take advantage of this fact and configure Safari to provide a different user agent string (such as Internet Explorer), and fool the site into letting you in.

To perform this trick, you must first configure Safari to display its normally hidden Debug menu. Here's how you do that:

1. **Choose Safari ➪ Preferences.** Safari displays its preferences.
2. **Click the Advanced tab.**
3. **Select the Show Develop menu in menu bar check box.**
4. **Close the Safari preferences.**

Safari now displays a Develop menu, which contains lots of commands of great interest to programmers. For your purposes, you need to choose Develop ➪ User Agent to see a list of user agent strings, as shown in Figure 11.17. Choose the string you want to use and then try accessing the site. If you still don't get in, keep trying different user agents.

When you're done with the site, choose Develop ➪ User Agent ➪ Default (Automatically Chosen) to reinstate the default user agent setting.

**11.17** With the Develop menu in place, the User Agent command presents a list of user agent strings you can use to fool a site into letting Safari in.

# Your bookmarks are in Internet Explorer

If you're switching from Windows to MacBook Air, you might be wondering if you have to give up all of your carefully stored Internet Explorer favorites as part of the deal. No way! As long as you still have access to your Windows machine, you can export your favorites from Internet Explorer and import them as bookmarks into Safari.

First, follow these steps to export your Internet Explorer favorites to a file:

1.  **On your Windows PC, launch Internet Explorer.**

2.  **Start the Import/Export Wizard.**

    - **Internet Explorer 8 and 9.** Click Favorites, and then click Add to Favorites menu (or press Alt+Z). Then click Import and Export.

    - **Internet Explorer 7.** Click the Add to Favorites icon (or press Alt+Z). Then click Import and Export.

    - **Earlier versions of Internet Explorer.** Choose File ➪ Import and Export.

3.  **Tell Internet Explorer you want to export your favorites.**

    - **Internet Explorer 8 and 9.** Select the Export to a File option and click Next. Select the Favorites check box and then click Next.

    - **Earlier versions of Internet Explorer.** Click Next and then click Export Favorites. Click Next.

4. **Click the Favorites folder (see Figure 11.18), and then click Next.** The Export Favorites Destination dialog appears.

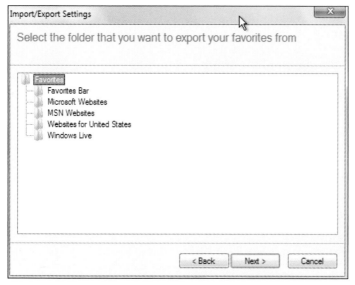

11.18 Select the Favorites folder to export all your Internet Explorer favorites.

5. **Choose a location for the export file.**

   • **Windows PC and Mac on the same network.** Save the favorites file in a folder that's shared on the network.

   • **Windows PC and Mac aren't on the same network.** Insert a USB flash drive into the Windows PC and save the favorites file to the flash drive.

6. **Click Next.** Internet Explorer exports the favorites to a file.

7. **Click Finish.**

Now you're ready to import your Internet Explorer favorites into Safari by following these steps:

1. **In Safari, choose File ⇨ Import Bookmarks.** The Import Bookmarks dialog appears.

2. **Open the folder that contains the favorites file you exported earlier from Internet Explorer.**

   • **Windows PC and Mac on the same network.** Open the shared network folder that contains the favorites file.

   • **Windows PC and Mac aren't on the same network.** Insert the USB flash drive that contains the favorites file.

3. **Click the favorites file.** In most cases, the file is named bookmark.htm.

4. **Click Import.** Safari adds the Internet Explorer favorites as bookmarks.

# You Can't Specify a Different Time Zone for an iCal Event

iCal assumes that all of your events happen in your present time zone. This is a reasonable assumption because for most of us our appointments, meetings, and other events happen locally. If you travel, however, it's quite possible that you might need to schedule events that occur in a different time zone.

To do this, you need to configure iCal to work with different time zones. Follow these steps:

1. **Choose iCal ➪ Preferences.** The iCal preferences appear.

2. **Click the Advanced pane.**

3. **Select the Turn on time zone support check box.**

4. **Close the iCal preferences.**

iCal adds a time zone menu to the upper-right corner of the window, as shown in Figure 11.19. To schedule an appointment in a different time zone, use the menu to select the new time zone, and then schedule your appointment using the correct time in that zone.

For example, if the event occurs at 9:00 AM in the other time zone, schedule the event for 9:00 AM. When you change back to your current time zone, iCal automatically adjusts the events to local time.

**11.19** When you enable time zone support in iCal, the program adds a time zone menu to the upper-right corner of the window.

**Genius** You can change the time zone for individual events. Double-click the event you want to change, and then click Edit. Click the Time Zone menu. Click the new time zone you want to use for the event and then click Done.

# How Do I Solve Specific Hardware Problems?

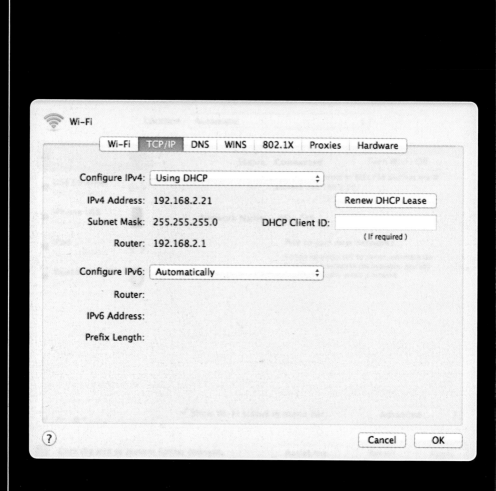

Wi-Fi

| Wi-Fi | TCP/IP | DNS | WINS | 802.1X | Proxies | Hardware |

Configure IPv4: Using DHCP

IPv4 Address: 192.168.2.21

Renew DHCP Lease

Subnet Mask: 255.255.255.0

DHCP Client ID:

( If required )

Router: 192.168.2.1

Configure IPv6: Automatically

Router:

IPv6 Address:

Prefix Length:

Cancel       OK

Even in the streamlined, lightweight, look-ma-no-moving-parts world of MacBook Air, devices sometimes behave strangely (or not at all). The generic troubleshooting and repair techniques that I cover in the past couple of chapters can solve all kinds of problems. However, there are always specific problems that require specific solutions. This chapter takes you through a few of the most common ones.

# MacBook Air Won't Start

Few problems are as frustrating as a MacBook Air that can't get on its feet. Here are some ideas for troubleshooting this most vexing problem:

- **Check your connections.** If MacBook Air won't even turn on (and the power cord isn't connected), the battery is probably drained. Connect the power cord and try powering up. If MacBook Air still won't start, make sure the power cord is properly connected at both ends. The LED on the connector that plugs into MacBook Air should be either green (indicating that the battery is fully charged) or amber (indicating that the battery is charging). Also, if the power cord is plugged into a power bar or surge protector, make sure that device is turned on. If the device has a reset switch, press that switch.

- **Remove all nonessential devices.** Disconnect everything from MacBook Air. If it starts successfully, one of the disconnected devices is likely the culprit. Reconnect the devices one at a time, restarting each one after you connect it. If after connecting one of the devices MacBook Air refuses to start, that last device is the problem.

- **Try a Safe Mode boot and then restart.** One of the things a Safe Mode boot (described in Chapter 10) does is delete the cache that MacBook Air uses for storing fonts to improve performance. If that cache gets corrupted, it could cause start-up headaches. Trashing the cache might do the trick.

- **Repair the hard drive.** A hard drive problem could be causing your start-up woes. Boot to a secondary device to repair it (as described in Chapter 10).

- **Repair hard drive permissions.** Improper permissions aren't likely to cause a start-up failure, but it's not out of the realm of possibility. Boot to a secondary device to repair them (see Chapter 10).

- **Reset the parameter random access memory (PRAM).** The PRAM holds data like virtual memory and the hard drive cache. It also holds settings, such as the speaker volume and monitor resolution. If any of these values is corrupted, it could prevent MacBook Air from starting. To reset the PRAM, press the MacBook Air power button and then immediately press and hold the Option, ⌘, P, and R keys. Keep the keys held down until MacBook Air restarts and you hear the start-up chime for the second time.

- **Reset MacBook Air's hard drive as the start-up device.** If you see a flashing question mark when you start MacBook Air, the most likely problem is that it can't find the hard drive. To fix this, hold down the Option key while you reboot MacBook Air. In the list of start-up devices that appears, choose Macintosh HD. If you don't see an icon for Macintosh HD, choose Recovery HD instead. When the Mac OS X Utilities application loads, choose Utilities ⇨ Terminal to load the Terminal application. At the prompt type the following command and then press Return:

```
bless -mount "Volumes/Macintosh HD" -setBoot
```

For versions of OS X prior to Lion, insert the Mac OS X Install USB flash drive, and then restart. Press and hold C until you see the Apple logo to ensure that MacBook Air boots to the flash drive. Press Return in the initial screen to load the Mac OS X Installer. Choose Utilities ⇨ Startup Disk and click the Macintosh HD icon. Click Restart and then click Restart again when the application asks you to confirm.

# MacBook Air Says You Don't Have Enough Memory

MacBook Air comes with 2GB or 4GB of RAM, so it's unlikely to run out of memory very often. However, it can happen — particularly if you work with large files or many programs at once. Here are some things to try if MacBook Air is low on RAM:

- **Close large files.** If you have any extremely large files open, try closing them.

**Genius**

One common cause for low RAM on a Mac is when you have a number of applications running that you don't know about. How can that happen? One way is to think you've shut down an application because you closed that application's window, but the application remains in memory. Check the Dock and look for icons of the applications that you thought you'd closed. If you see any open apps, right-click the icon and then click Quit.

- **Close running applications.** Shut down any applications that you don't need.
- **Log out.** This should help a lot because it shuts down all of your open applications and documents.
- **Restart MacBook Air.** This is the ultimate way to clear out the RAM and get a fresh start.

# MacBook Air Runs Slowly

All Mac users want their Macs to be as speedy as the first day they got them, but sometimes that's not the case. If you find that MacBook Air has that molasses-in-January thing going, you can try a few things before you start pulling your hair out in clumps.

233

# Sudden slowdown

If the slowdown is a recent and relatively sudden phenomenon, it suggests one of the following remedies:

- **Shut down some running programs.** It's possible that you have too many programs running. This causes MacBook Air to constantly swap data between RAM and the hard drive's virtual memory, which can really slow things down.

- **Look for a runaway application in Activity Monitor.** In Finder, choose Applications ⇨ Utilities ⇨ Activity Monitor and look for a process that's using up a large percentage of the CPU time. If you see one, shut it down (click the process and then click Quit Process).

- **Uninstall a recently installed program.** If the slowdown coincided with a recent program installation, try uninstalling the program by dragging it to the Trash.

- **Repair the hard drive.** Some hard drive file system problems can cause system-wide slowdowns. Try a disk repair (as described in Chapter 10) and see if that fixes the problem.

# Gradual slowdown

If MacBook Air has been getting slower gradually, the usual cause is the accumulation over time of programs, widgets, add-ons, and other bric-a-brac that slowly take their toll on system performance. Here are some ideas that might alleviate the slowdown:

- **Applications.** Installed applications often load files at start-up, so they may take up precious resources even when you're not using them. Uninstall any application that you no longer use.

- **Login items.** Remove as many as you can, as described in Chapter 7.

- **Dashboard widgets.** Disable or remove any widgets that you don't use.

- **Browser add-ons.** These take up memory, so get rid of any you really don't need.

# Your Mouse or Keyboard Doesn't Work

Your MacBook Air is a slick, sleek machine, but in the end it's just that: a machine. This means that it's just as dumb and helpless as any other collection of transistors and relays, so it can't do all that much on its own. No, your MacBook Air needs you, and in particular it needs you to use a keyboard and mouse to input commands, select options, and generally just give MacBook Air its marching orders.

Being the boss of your MacBook Air gets a lot harder when your tools of command — the keyboard and mouse — don't work. Fortunately the MacBook Air's built-in keyboard and trackpad are rock-solid components that only rarely break down, but that doesn't mean they don't cause other types of problems.

# You can't press Tab to navigate a dialog

It's usually easiest to navigate a dialog using your mouse to select a check box or option, choose a list item, or enter a text box. However, some dialogs lend themselves to easier keyboard navigation, where you press Tab to move forward through the controls, or Shift+Tab to move backward. Or, I should say, dialogs that consist only of lists and text boxes lend themselves to easier keyboard navigation because, by default, Mac OS X doesn't Tab (or Shift+Tab) into other types of controls: check boxes, option buttons, pop-ups, sliders, tabs, and so on.

This is odd and frustrating behavior, but you can solve it with a simple keyboard command: Press Control+F7 (remember to also hold down the Fn key to get the true F7 key; see the next section). This feature is called Full Keyboard Access, and it means you can now Tab (or Shift+Tab) into any dialog control. Note, however, that in many cases you're only highlighting the control; you're not selecting it or choosing it. To do that, press the spacebar.

# You can't use F1, F2 (and so on) as standard function keys

As you might know, the keys along the top row of your MacBook Air have been preassigned special features. For example, F1 dims the screen, F3 displays Mission Control, and F7 pauses and plays the current iTunes track. When you want to use one of these keys as a standard function key, you must hold down the Fn key at the same time. For example, to toggle Full Keyboard Access, as described in the previous section, you must press Fn+Control+F7; if you just press Control+F7, you only pause or restart the current iTunes track.

If you use F1 to F12 as standard function keys more than as special function keys, having to remember to hold down Fn each time is annoying, particularly when you forget and end up launching Mission Control or Dashboard. Fortunately, you can reverse the way that Mac OS X treats these keys. That is, you can use F1 through F12 as standard function keys and to use a key as a special function, you must hold down Fn. Here's how:

1. **Click System Preferences in the Dock.** The System Preferences window appears.

2. **Click Keyboard to open the keyboard preferences.**

3. **Click the Keyboard tab.**

4. **Select the Use all F1, F2, etc. keys as standard function keys, as shown in Figure 12.1.**

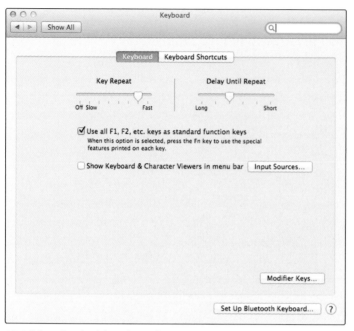

**12.1** Select the check box shown here to use F1 through F12 as standard function keys.

# You can't right-click the MacBook Air trackpad

Right-clicking something is a useful technique for displaying an object's shortcut menu, which is a list of the object's most common — or, given the current program context, its most useful — commands. How frustrating, then, if you find that you can't right-click anything on the MacBook Air trackpad.

As a first troubleshooting step, try pointing at the object you want to right-click. Now tap or click the trackpad using two fingers. This is the default method for *secondary clicking* (as Apple prefers to call right-clicking). To change this to a single-click, or if nothing happened even when you used a two-finger tap or click, follow these steps:

1. **Click System Preferences in the Dock to open the System Preferences window.**

2. **Click Trackpad.** The trackpad preferences appear.

3. **Click the Point & Click tab.**

4. **Select the Secondary click check box.**

5. **See the Secondary click list to choose Click in bottom right corner, as shown in Figure 12.2.**

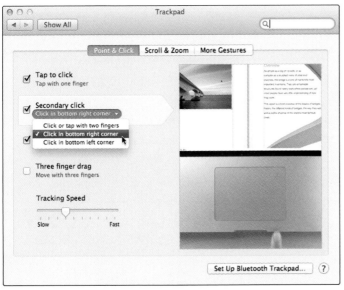

12.2 Select the Secondary click check box and then choose Click in bottom right corner.

# Your external mouse or keyboard doesn't work

The good news is, if you're using an external mouse or keyboard with MacBook Air and either stops working, you're not stuck. You can always revert to the built-in mouse or keyboard. However, I'm guessing that you still want your external mouse and keyboard back up and running. Here are some suggested remedies to try in the face of recalcitrant input devices:

- **Turn it on.** If you're using a Bluetooth mouse or keyboard, make sure it's turned on.
- **Make the device discoverable.** If you're using a Bluetooth mouse or keyboard, press the button or switch that makes the device discoverable, which often helps MacBook Air find the device and reestablish a connection.
- **Pair the device again.** If you're using a Bluetooth mouse or keyboard, try pairing the device and MacBook Air once again.
- **Change the batteries.** If you're using a Bluetooth mouse or keyboard, try a fresh set of batteries.

237

- **Wait for a bit.** Sometimes it only seems as though the mouse or keyboard is stuck when, in fact, it's actually waiting for some process to finish. Leave the devices be for a bit (particularly the keyboard; banging away on the keys won't solve anything) and then see if they respond.

- **Disconnect and reconnect.** If you're using a USB mouse or keyboard, disconnect it, wait a short while (5 or 10 seconds is fine), and then reconnect.

- **Try a different port.** If you're using a USB mouse or keyboard with a USB hub, disconnect the device and plug it into a different USB port on the hub. If the device works now, your USB port may be faulty.

- **Connect directly to the MacBook Air.** If you're using a USB mouse or keyboard and the device is attached to a USB hub, disconnect it from the hub and connect it to the USB port on MacBook Air. If the device works now, your USB hub might be wonky.

- **Try another device.** If you have a spare mouse or keyboard lying around, try connecting it to MacBook Air. If it works, the original mouse or keyboard is broken.

- **Restart.** Rebooting MacBook Air might just solve the problem.

# Your Display Is Garbled

If your display suddenly goes haywire, a number of things could be the problem, but the following five are the most common:

- **It's a temporary glitch.** This is the usual cause of a wonky display, and you solve it by restarting MacBook Air. Because you can't see the Mac desktop, your mouse is no good to you, so you need to use the keyboard. First press Shift+⌘+Q to log out. If that doesn't work, press and hold the Control and ⌘ keys and then press the power button to force MacBook Air to restart.

- **For an external display, there's a loose connection.** If MacBook Air is connected to an external display, check the connection on the MacBook Air, on the monitor, and on both ends of the display adapter, if you're using one. If any connector is loose, plugging it in properly should fix the problem right away. If not, turn the monitor off and then back on.

- **The display is using improper settings.** If your display somehow gets set to a resolution that it can't handle, you see a distorted screen image. To solve this problem, restart MacBook Air in Safe Mode and click System Preferences in the Dock. Click the Displays icon, and then click an item in the Resolutions list.

- **The display shows white on black instead of the usual black on white.** This is actually a feature of the Mac's Universal Access preferences. You (or another user) may have turned it on accidentally. Click System Preferences in the Dock and click the Universal Access icon. Click Seeing and then select the Black on White option. Note, too, that you can toggle between the settings by pressing Control+Option+⌘+8.

- **The external display's driver software is corrupted.** In this case, you either need to reinstall the driver software from the disc that came with the display, or you need to download the driver from the display manufacturer's website and install it. In either case, you need to restart MacBook Air in Safe Mode.

# Your MacBook Air SuperDrive Won't Work

The lack of an optical drive in the original MacBook Air was a scandalous omission at the time, with many pundits seeing this as a critical flaw that would doom the new machine's prospects in the marketplace. Wrong! We're now several generations into the era of the MacBook Air, and now nobody even *mentions* the lack of an optical drive, much less grumbles about it. However, an optical is still an occasionally useful tool, and the made-for-MacBook Air SuperDrive is an excellent choice. This section presents a couple of fixes for some fortunately rare SuperDrive woes.

## SuperDrive won't accept a disc

When you insert a disc into your MacBook Air SuperDrive, it normally grabs the disc and seats it inside the drive. MacBook Air then shows a desktop icon for the drive a few seconds later. However, you may find that your MacBook Air SuperDrive doesn't accept a disc. That is, even if you insert the disc as far as it will go, the drive doesn't grab it and no disc icon appears on the desktop.

Although it's possible the MacBook Air SuperDrive is defective, a much more likely explanation is that the drive is plugged into a USB hub. Unfortunately, that's a no-no with the MacBook Air SuperDrive. It needs to be connected directly to MacBook Air's USB port. The drive gets its electrical power only from that port, not from a USB hub port.

## You can't eject a disc

Few things are as frustrating as a CD or DVD that simply will not eject, whether you press the Eject key or ⌘+E, drag the disc icon to the Trash, or choose File ➪ Eject. This is a surprisingly (some would say distressingly) common problem. However, there are a lot of things you can try and one of them almost always works. If you have an external optical drive — such as the MacBook Air SuperDrive — connected to MacBook Air, try these solutions:

- **Check the external drive connection.** If you're using the MacBook Air SuperDrive, make sure it's connected directly to MacBook Air's USB port, and not to a USB hub. If you're using another type of external optical drive, make sure it's connected to MacBook Air or the USB hub, and that it's plugged in and turned on.

- **Eject from iTunes.** When the standard eject methods don't work, it's surprising how often the iTunes eject is successful. Launch iTunes and then click the Eject button in the lower-right corner of the window.

- **Eject from Disk Utility.** If iTunes can't eject the disc, there's a very good chance that Disk Utility can. In Finder, choose Go ⇨ Utilities and then double-click Disk Utility. Click the disc and then click the Eject button in the toolbar (or choose File ⇨ Eject, or press ⌘+E).

**Note**   When trying to eject the disc at start-up, be sure to press and hold the left button of MacBook Air's built-in trackpad. If you try to use a wireless mouse for this, it won't work.

- **Eject the disc at start-up.** Restart MacBook Air and wait until you hear the chime that announces system start-up. Press and hold the left mouse button until the disc ejects. If you get as far as the login screen or the desktop, release the mouse button because the technique didn't work.

- **Eject the disc manually.** If you're using an external optical drive other than the MacBook Air SuperDrive, you may be able to eject the disc manually. Just below the disc tray, look for a tiny hole. Grab a paper clip, straighten it out, and then poke one end of it into the hole. If you do this with enough pressure, the drive tray will open slightly, and you can then pull it the rest of the way out.

# You Have Trouble Accessing a Wireless Network

Wireless networking adds a whole new set of potential snags to your troubleshooting chores because of problems such as interference and device ranges. Here's a list of a few troubleshooting items that you should check to solve any wireless connectivity problems you're having with MacBook Air:

- **Make sure Wi-Fi is on.** If you see the Wi-Fi status icon in the menu bar, click it. If you see Wi-Fi: Off, click Turn Wi-Fi On. If you don't see the Wi-Fi status icon, open System Preferences, click Network, and then click Wi-Fi. If the Status value is Off, click Turn Wi-Fi On.

- **Toggle Wi-Fi off and on.** If Wi-Fi has gone a bit haywire, resetting it sometimes helps. Click the Wi-Fi status icon in the menu bar and click Turn Wi-Fi Off. Click the Wi-Fi status icon again, and then click Turn Wi-Fi On. Alternatively, open System Preferences, click Network, click Wi-Fi, and then click Turn Wi-Fi On.

- **Reestablish the connection.** If Wi-Fi is on, check the Wi-Fi status icon. If you see gray bars instead of black bars, it means that MacBook Air isn't currently connected to any network. Click the Wi-Fi icon and then click the network you want to use. If you don't see the Wi-Fi status icon, open System Preferences, click Network, and then click Wi-Fi. In the Network Name menu, click the network you want to join.

- **Renew the lease.** When you connect to a wireless network, the access point gives MacBook Air a Dynamic Host Control Protocol (DHCP) lease that allows it to access the network. You can often solve connectivity problems by renewing that lease. Open System Preferences, click Network, click Wi-Fi, and then click Advanced. Click the TCP/IP tab, as shown in Figure 12.3, and then click Renew DHCP Lease. Wait until you see a new value in the IPv4 Address field, and then click OK.

12.3 In the advanced Wi-Fi settings, click Renew DHCP Lease to get a fresh lease on (wireless network) life.

● **Reboot and power cycle devices.** Reset your hardware by performing the following tasks, in order: Restart MacBook Air; power cycle the wireless access point; and power cycle the broadband modem.

**Genius**

You should also keep MacBook Air and the wireless access point well away from a microwave oven. Microwaves can jam wireless signals.

● **Look for interference.** Devices that use the 2.4 GHz radio frequency (RF) band, such as baby monitors and cordless phones, can play havoc with wireless signals. Try either moving or turning off such devices if they're near MacBook Air or the wireless access point.

● **Check your range.** If you're not getting a signal (or a you're getting a weak signal), it could be that MacBook Air is too far away from the access point. You usually can't get much farther than about 230 feet from an access point before the signal begins to degrade. Either move closer to the access point or, if it has one, turn on the access point's range booster feature. You could also install a wireless range extender.

● **Update the access point firmware.** The access point firmware is the internal program that the access point uses to perform its various chores. Access point manufacturers frequently update their firmware to fix bugs, so you should see if an updated version of it is available. See your device documentation to learn how this works.

● **Reset the router.** As a last resort, reset the router to its default factory settings (see the device documentation to learn how to do this). Note that if you do this you must set up your network from scratch.

# Your Sound Isn't Working

Whether you're using the built-in MacBook Air speaker or external speakers connected to MacBook Air's audio output jack, if you're getting no sound, you're getting no joy from applications such as iTunes, QuickTime, and GarageBand. Here are a few things to try:

● **Check the sound volume.** You'd be surprised how often sound problems are really just a volume issue because someone has turned the MacBook Air volume down to its lowest level. Check the volume icon in the menu bar. If you don't see any "waves" coming out of the speaker, click the volume icon. Then click and drag the slider to turn up the volume. If you don't see the volume icon, open System Preferences, click Sound, and then click the Output tab, shown in Figure 12.4. Deselect the Mute check box, and then use the Output volume slider to set the system volume.

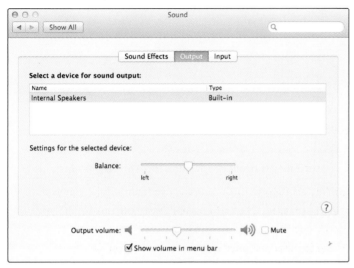

12.4 In the Sound preferences, use the Output tab to set the volume.

- **Change the output device.** If you have multiple sound output devices — say external speakers or Bluetooth headphones — it's possible that MacBook Air is trying to output the sound to a device that's not currently on or connected. Open System Preferences, click Sound, and then click the Output tab. In the Select a device for sound output list (see Figure 12.4), click either Internal Speakers or another device that you know is connected.

- **Check the output device.** If you're using external speakers, make sure that they are plugged in to an AC outlet and turned on. Also check the connection to MacBook Air. If you're using Bluetooth speakers, make sure the device is discoverable and that it has been paired with MacBook Air.

- **Get Windows Media Components for QuickTime.** If you're trying to play files, such as audio files in the WMA (Windows Media Audio) format, you won't get very far. Mac OS X doesn't support that format, as it is proprietary to Microsoft. Fortunately, Microsoft offers a QuickTime add-on called Windows Media Components for QuickTime, which extends QuickTime so that it can play Windows Media files. Visit the following page to download the add-on:

windows.microsoft.com/en-US/windows/products/windows-media-player/wmcomponents

# Appendix A

# MacBook Air Online Resources

The Internet is chock-full of Mac-related sites, many of which are exceptionally good and reflect the passion that most Mac users feel toward their beloved machines. This appendix lists a few of the best sites for great information on all things Mac — from tips to troubleshooting and more. Most of these sites have been online for a while, so they should still be up and running when you read this. That said, things do change constantly on the web, so don't be too surprised if one or two have gone sneakers up.

## Official Apple Sites

If you like your information straight from the horse's mouth, here are a few useful Mac sites maintained by the good geeks at Apple.

### www.apple.com/mac/

This is your starting point for Mac-related stuff on the Apple site. You'll find the latest Mac news, the top downloads, and the latest Mac ads (always a great time-waster).

### www.apple.com/macbookair/

The official Apple home of MacBook Air.

### www.apple.com/support/hardware/

Head here for user guides, software updates, how-to articles, and troubleshooting tips for MacBook Air.

# http://discussions.apple.com

This site contains Apple's discussion forums, where you can talk to other Mac fans and ask questions.

# More Mac Sites

If you feel like surfing off the beaten track, there are plenty of third-party Mac sites maintained by Mac enthusiasts.

# http://tidbits.com

The best place to find news and commentary related to what's going on in the Mac universe.

# www.download.cnet.com/Mac

This site has a huge selection of Mac software downloads.

# www.macfixit.com

Troubleshooting solutions for your Mac.

# www.macintouch.com

You'll find the latest news from the world of Mac here.

# www.macosxhints.com

This site provides a massive database of user-generated Mac tips.

# www.macrumors.com

More news and more than a few rumors about the Mac.

# www.macworld.com

Go to this site to find articles, tips, and discussions from the publisher of *Macworld* magazine.

# www.tucows.com/Macintosh

This site has thousands of Mac-related software downloads.

# www.ultimatemac.com

Go to this site for Mac news, tips, troubleshooting, software reviews, and much more.

# www.xlr8yourmac.com

You'll find hundreds of great tips and how-to articles for getting more out of your Mac here.

# Appendix B

# MacBook Air Shortcut Keys

**Although** MacBook Air was built with the mouse in mind, it comes with lots of keyboard shortcuts. These can save you time and make many operations easier and faster. The sections in this appendix summarize the most useful MacBook Air keyboard shortcuts.

## Start-up Shortcuts

Table B.1 details shortcuts you can use for alternate booting techniques.

**Table B.1** Startup Shortcuts

| Shortcut | Description |
|----------|-------------|
| C | Press and hold to boot from the inserted CD or DVD |
| T | Press and hold to invoke FireWire Target Disk mode |
| Option | Press and hold to display the Startup Manager |
| Shift | Press and hold before the Apple screen comes up to boot into Safe Mode |
| Shift | Press and hold after the Apple screen comes up but before login to bypass login items |
| Shift | Press and hold after login to boot into Safe Login Mode |

# Restart and Shutdown Shortcuts

Table B.2 gives you some different options for the various dialogs you see when you restart or shut down your MacBook Air.

**Table B.2** Restart and Shutdown Shortcuts

| Shortcut | Description |
| --- | --- |
| Shift+⌘+Q | Log out (with confirmation dialog) |
| Option+Shift+⌘+Q | Log out (without confirmation dialog) |
| Control+Eject | Display the Restart/Sleep/Shut Down confirmation dialog |
| Power | Display the Restart/Sleep/Shut Down confirmation dialog |
| Option+⌘+Eject | Put MacBook Air into Sleep Mode (without confirmation dialog) |
| Control+⌘+Eject | Restart MacBook Air (without confirmation dialog, but you can save changes in open documents) |
| Control+Option+⌘+Eject | Shut down MacBook Air (without confirmation dialog, but you can save changes in open documents) |
| Control+⌘+Power | Force MacBook Air to restart (without confirmation dialog, and you can't save changes in open documents) |
| Power | Press and hold to force MacBook Air to shut down (without confirmation dialog, and you can't save changes in open documents) |

# Application Shortcuts

Table B.3 shows you how to cycle through your current application's icons, how to open the application's preferences, and how to maneuver through windows without using your mouse.

**Table B.3** Application Shortcuts

| Shortcut | Description |
|---|---|
| ⌘+Tab | Cycle forward through active application icons with each press of the Tab key; release ⌘ to switch to the selected application |
| Shift+⌘+Tab | Cycle backward through active application icons with each press of the Tab key; release ⌘ to switch to the selected application |
| ⌘+` | Cycle forward through the current application's open windows |
| Shift+⌘+` | Cycle backward through the current application's open windows |
| ⌘+, | Open the current application's preferences |
| ⌘+H | Hide the current application |
| Option+⌘+H | Hide all applications except the current one |
| ⌘+M | Minimize the current window to the Dock |
| Option+⌘+M | Minimize all windows in active applications to the Dock |
| ⌘+Q | Quit the current application |
| Option+⌘+Esc | Display the Force Quit Applications window |

# Finder Shortcuts

Use the shortcuts in Table B.4 to switch Finder window views, open a new Finder window, eject a disc, duplicate files and folders, maneuver through Finder's sidebar, or manage your Trash.

**Table B.4** Finder Shortcuts

| Shortcut | Description |
|---|---|
| ⌘+1 | Switch the active window to Icons view |
| ⌘+2 | Switch the active window to List Flow view |
| ⌘+3 | Switch the active window to Columns view |
| ⌘+4 | Switch the active window to Cover Flow view |
| ⌘+A | Select all items in the current window |
| ⌘+D | Duplicate the selected item |
| ⌘+E | Eject the current disc |
| ⌘+F | Display the Find dialog |
| ⌘+I | Display the Get Info window for the selected item |
| ⌘+J | Display the View options |
| ⌘+L | Create an alias for the selected item |
| ⌘+N | Open a new Finder window |
| ⌘+O | Open the selected item |
| ⌘+R | Show the original item for the current alias |
| ⌘+T | Add the current item to the sidebar |
| ⌘+W | Close the current Finder window |
| Shift+⌘+A | Go to the Applications folder |
| Shift+⌘+C | Go to the Computer folder |
| Shift+⌘+D | Go to the Desktop folder |
| Shift+⌘+G | Display the Go to Folder dialog |
| Shift+⌘+H | Go to the Home folder |
| Shift+⌘+I | Go to the iDisk folder |
| Shift+⌘+K | Go to the Network folder |
| Shift+⌘+N | Create a new folder in the current Finder window |
| Option+⌘+N | Create a new Smart Folder in the current Finder window |
| Shift+⌘+U | Go to the Utilities folder |
| Option+⌘+W | Close all open Finder windows |
| ⌘+Delete | Move the selected item to the Trash |
| Shift+⌘+Delete | Empty the Trash (with the confirmation dialog) |
| Option+Shift+⌘+Delete | Empty the Trash (without the confirmation dialog) |

# Safari Shortcuts

Table B.5 details the shortcuts you can use to maneuver through Safari windows, manage your bookmarks, send e-mails, and perform Google searches.

**Table B.5** Safari Shortcuts

| Shortcut | Description |
| --- | --- |
| ⌘+I | E-mail the contents of the current page |
| ⌘+L | Select the Address bar text |
| ⌘+N | Open a new window |
| ⌘+O | Open a file |
| ⌘+R | Reload the current page |
| ⌘+T | Open a new tab |
| ⌘+W | Close the current tab |
| ⌘+*n* | Open the *n*th item on the Bookmarks bar, where *n* is a number between one and nine |
| ⌘+} | Select the next tab |
| ⌘+{ | Select the previous tab |
| ⌘+. | Stop loading the current page |
| ⌘++ | Make the text bigger on the current page |
| ⌘+0 | Make the text normal size on the current page |
| ⌘+- | Make the text smaller on the current page |
| ⌘+D | Add the current page to the Bookmarks |
| Option+⌘+D | Add the current page to the Bookmarks (without the Bookmark dialog) |
| Option+⌘+B | Display the Bookmarks window |
| Option+⌘+L | Display the Downloads window |
| ⌘+[ | Navigate back |
| ⌘+] | Navigate forward |
| Shift+⌘+H | Navigate to the Home page |
| Shift+⌘+T | Toggle the Tab bar on and off (works only if you have one tab open) |
| Shift+⌘+W | Close the current window |
| Shift+⌘+I | E-mail a link to the current page |
| Shift+⌘+K | Toggle pop-up blocking on and off |
| Shift+⌘+L | Run a Google search on the selected text |
| ⌘+Return | Open the Address bar URL in a background tab |

*(continued)*

## Table B.5 continued

| Shortcut | Description |
|----------|-------------|
| Shift+⌘+Return | Open the Address bar URL in a foreground tab |
| ⌘ | Click a link to open it in a background tab |
| Shift+⌘ | Click a link to open it in a foreground tab |
| Option+⌘ | Click a link to open it in a background window |
| Shift+Option+⌘ | Click a link to open it in a foreground window |
| Option+⌘+Return | Open the address bar URL in a background window |
| Shift+Option+⌘+Return | Open the address bar URL in a foreground window |

# Miscellaneous Shortcuts

Use the shortcuts in Table B.6 to cut, copy, and paste materials, undo recent actions, manage the Dock, and capture screenshots.

## Table B.6 Miscellaneous Shortcuts

| Shortcut | Description |
|----------|-------------|
| ⌘+X | Cut the selected objects or data |
| ⌘+C | Copy the selected objects or data |
| ⌘+V | Paste the most recently cut or copied objects or data |
| ⌘+Z | Undo the most recent action |
| Option+Volume up/down/mute | Display the Sound preferences |
| Option+Brightness up/down | Display the Display preferences |
| F12 | Press and hold to eject an inserted disc |
| Fn+Control+F2 | Give keyboard control to the menu bar |
| Fn+Control+F3 | Give keyboard control to the Dock |
| Option+⌘+D | Toggle Dock hiding on and off |
| Shift+⌘+3 | Capture an image of the screen |
| Shift+⌘+4 | Drag the mouse to capture an image of the selected area of the screen |
| Shift+⌘+4 | Press spacebar and then click an object to capture an image of that object |

## Table B.7  iTunes Playback Shortcuts

| Shortcut | Description |
| --- | --- |
| Return | Start playing the chosen song |
| Spacebar | Pause/Play the current song |
| Option+⌘+Right arrow | Fast-forward the current song |
| Option+⌘+Left arrow | Rewind the current song |
| Right arrow | Skip to the next song |
| Left arrow | Skip to the beginning of the current song; press again to skip to the previous song |
| Option+Right arrow | Skip to the next album |
| Option+Left arrow | Skip to the previous album |
| ⌘+Up arrow | Increase the volume |
| ⌘+Down arrow | Decrease the volume |
| Option+⌘+Down arrow | Mute/unmute the volume |
| ⌘+E | Eject an audio CD |

# Appendix C

# MacBook Air Multi-Touch Gestures

**MacBook Air's** trackpad is certainly useful for moving the mouse, clicking things, and dragging objects from here to there. However, the trackpad is much more versatile than all that because it supports a nifty piece of technology called *Multi-Touch*: the ability to sense and react to two or more fingers touching the trackpad at the same time. This enables you to manipulate screen objects with unprecedented versatility, and all you have to know is a few gestures that use one, two, three, and sometimes even four fingers.

## One-finger Gestures

Here's a list of the one-finger gestures supported by the MacBook Air trackpad:

- **Pointing.** Slide a finger along the trackpad to move the mouse pointer.
- **Tapping.** Move the mouse pointer over an object and then lightly touch the trackpad.
- **Clicking.** Move the mouse pointer over an object and then press the trackpad.

**Note**

In most cases, there's not much difference between tapping and clicking, because both are used to select objects, toggle check boxes and option buttons, choose dialog command buttons, and so on.

# Two-finger Gestures

Here are some useful gestures you can perform using two fingers on the MacBook Air trackpad:

- **Dragging.** Move the mouse pointer over an object, use one finger to click and hold down the trackpad, and slide a second finger along the trackpad to move the object.
- **Right-clicking.** Move the mouse pointer over an object and then tap or click using two fingers.
- **Scrolling.** Tap or click inside the window you want to scroll, then slide two fingers along the trackpad to move the window content in the direction you move your fingers.

**Genius**

Mac OS X Lion makes a crucial distinction between "scrolling a window" and "moving a window's content." For example, if you're at the top of a web page and you want to see more of the page, you can either scroll down or move the content up. By default, Lion assumes the latter, so you slide two fingers up to see more of the page. If you prefer to scroll down, open System Preferences, click Trackpad, click Scroll & Zoom, and then deselect the Scroll direction: natural check box.

- **Zooming.** Place two fingers on the trackpad and spread them apart to zoom in, or pinch them together to zoom out.
- **Smart zooming.** Double-tap the trackpad to expand a photo to fill the screen; double-tap again to zoom back out.
- **Rotating.** Position the mouse pointer over an image, place two fingers lightly on the trackpad, and then rotate the fingers in a circle. MacBook Air rotates the image in the same direction as your fingers.
- **Navigating pages.** In an application that contains multiple items or pages, slide two fingers to the right to view the next item, or slide two fingers to the left to view the previous item. If the application's items or pages are displayed vertically, slide two fingers down or up to navigate the items.

# Three-finger Gestures

Here's a list of the three-finger gestures you can use on the MacBook Air trackpad:

- **Looking up a word in the Dictionary.** Select the word (double-tap it), then double-tap the trackpad using three fingers.

- **Dragging with three fingers.** Move the mouse pointer over an object, place three fingers on the trackpad, and then slide all three fingers at once to move the object.

**Genius**
Three-finger dragging is turned off by default. To turn it on, open System Preferences, click Trackpad, click Point & Click, and then select the Three finger drag check box.

# Four-finger Gestures

Here's a list of the four-finger gestures you can use on the MacBook Air trackpad:

- **Opening Launchpad.** Place four fingers on the trackpad and pinch them together.

- **Opening Mission Control.** Place four fingers on the trackpad and swipe up. Swipe down with four fingers to close Mission Control.

- **Navigating full-screen applications.** Place four fingers on the trackpad and swipe left or right.

- **Showing the desktop.** Place four fingers on the trackpad and spread them apart.

- **Displaying an application's open windows.** Place four fingers on the trackpad and swipe down (this feature is called App Exposé). Swipe up with four fingers to return to the application's regular view.

**Genius**
App Exposé is turned off by default. To activate it, open System Preferences, click Trackpad, click More Gestures, and then select the App Exposé check box.

# Glossary

**access point** A networking device that enables two or more Macs to connect over a wireless network.

**ad hoc wireless network** See *computer-to-computer wireless network*.

**Bluetooth** A wireless networking technology that enables you to exchange data between two devices using radio frequencies when the devices are within range of each other (usually within about 10 meters).

**Bonjour** An Apple technology that scours the local network looking for other computers and devices that provide services, and then configures those services without requiring any input from you.

**bookmark** An Internet site saved in Safari so that you can access the site quickly in future browsing sessions.

**central processing unit** See *CPU*.

**computer-to-computer wireless network** A wireless network that doesn't use an access point. See also *infrastructure wireless network*.

**CPU** The chip inside MacBook Air that acts as the computer's control and command center. Also called the processor.

**deep discharge state** A battery condition where the battery can no longer hold a charge.

**defragmented** Describes a hard drive in which each file is stored in a single place on the drive. See also *fragmented*.

**discoverable** Describes a device that has its Bluetooth feature turned on so that other Bluetooth devices can connect to it.

**dual-link** A Digital Video Interface (DVI) cable that uses two transmitters. See also *single-link*.

**event** An appointment or meeting that you've scheduled in iCal.

**extended desktop mode** An external display mode in which MacBook Air's desktop is extended onto the external display. See also *video mirroring*.

**false positives** A legitimate e-mail message that has been marked as spam.

**female connector** A cable connector with holes. See also *male connector*.

**firewall** A security feature that monitors a computer's incoming connections to ensure that no unauthorized data makes it through.

**firmware** A small program that runs inside the device and controls its internal functions.

**fragmented** Describes a hard drive in which the files are broken into smaller chunks and spread around the drive. See also *defragmented*.

**Gbps** Gigabytes per second (billions of bits per second).

**group** A collection of Address Book contacts. See also *Smart Group*.

**HTML** See *Hypertext Markup Language*.

**Hypertext Markup Language** A collection of codes — called tags — that define the underlying structure of, and to some extent the formatting on, a web page.

**infrastructure wireless network** A standard wireless network that uses an access point. See also *computer-to-computer wireless network*.

**keychain** A list of saved passwords.

**login items** The applications, files, folders, network shares, and other items that start automatically when you sign in to your user account.

**male connector** A cable connector with pins. See also *female connector*.

**memory effect** The process where a battery loses capacity over time if you repeatedly recharge it without first fully discharging it.

**multithreading** Running two or more threads in a single program at the same time. See also *thread*.

**pair** To connect one Bluetooth device with another by typing a passkey.

**partition** A subset of a hard drive onto which you install an operating system (such as Mac OS X in one partition and Windows in another).

**permissions** A collection of settings that determine what users, or groups of users, can do with a file.

**piconet** An ad hoc wireless network created by two Bluetooth devices.

**port forwarding** Taking data that comes in to the router on a specific port and sending it to a specified computer on the network.

**power cycle** To turn a device off, wait a few seconds for its inner components to stop spinning, and then turn it back on.

**preferences** The options, settings, and other data you configure for MacBook Air via System Preferences.

**preferences file** A document that stores options and other data that you've entered using an application's Preferences command.

**private browsing** Surfing the web with Safari configured not to store sites on the history list, not to save search box text or AutoFill text, and where no files are added to the Downloads window.

**private IP address** The IP address of the router's network connection. See also *public IP address*.

**process**  A running instance of an executable program.

**processor**  See *CPU*.

**public IP address**  The IP address of the router's Internet connection as assigned by your Internet service provider. See also *private IP address*.

**recovery disk**  A USB flash drive or external hard drive that contains the same recovery tools as the Mac OS X Lion Recovery HD.

**remote DVD**  An optical drive on a network Mac or Windows PC that MacBook Air can access and use as a DVD drive.

**rich text**  Text that includes formatting features, such as fonts, colors, and styles.

**Safe Boot**  To start MacBook Air in Safe Mode.

**Safe Login**  A login that doesn't load any of your login items.

**Safe Mode**  A start-up mode where MacBook Air doesn't load most of its behind-the-scenes components.

**single-link**  A DVI cable that uses one transmitter. See also *dual-link*.

**S.M.A.R.T.**  Self-Monitoring Analysis and Reporting Technology. A technology that monitors a number of hard drive parameters, including spin-up time, drive temperature, drive errors, and bad sectors.

**Smart Group**  A collection of Address Book contacts where each member has one or more things in common. Also, where Address Book automatically adds or deletes members as you add, edit, and delete contacts. See also *group*.

**Smart Mailbox**  A Mail folder that consolidates all messages that meet one or more conditions. Also, where Mail automatically adds or deletes messages as you receive and delete them.

**SMTP server**  The Simple Mail Transport Protocol server that an Internet service provider uses to process outgoing e-mail messages.

**spinning wait cursor**  The rainbow-colored spinning cursor that appears when the system takes a long time to complete some task. Also called the spinning pizza and the spinning beach ball of death.

**swap file**  The area of virtual memory that MacBook Air is actually using.

**synchronization**  A process that ensures that data such as contacts, e-mail accounts, and events on MacBook Air is the same as the data on other devices, such as cell phones and PDAs.

**tamperproof Torx screw**  The type of screw used to secure the case of third- and fourth-generation MacBook Airs.

**thread**  A program task that can run independently of and, (usually) concurrently with, other tasks in the same program. See also *multithreading*.

**Universal Plug and Play**  A technology standard that enables a system, such as MacBook Air, to recognize, interrogate, and configure a hardware device.

**UPnP**  See *Universal Plug and Play*.

**user agent**  A string that a web browser uses to identify itself to a web server.

**user-installable** Describes a computer component that is fairly easy to remove and replace.

**vCard** A file that contains a person's contact information.

**video mirroring** An external display mode where the same image that appears on MacBook Air's main or built-in display also appears on the external display. See also *extended desktop mode*.

**virtual memory** Memory that MacBook Air can address beyond what is physically installed on the system by using a piece of your hard drive set up to emulate physical memory.

**web bug** An image that resides on a remote server and is added to an HTML-formatted e-mail message to prove that your e-mail address is legitimate.

**widget** A small program that runs in MacBook Air's Dashboard application.

**workflow** A script created with Automator that implements a series of actions where the data returned by one action is passed along to the next.

**zero out** To overwrite the free space in a hard drive with a series of 0s.

# Index

# The Genius is in.

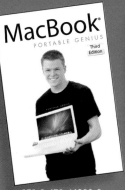
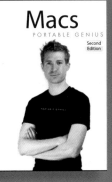